Relationship Goals
Michael Todd

Are you looking for lasting love? Get real about your objectives! Drawing from his popular sermon series, Todd equips you with the tools to build intimate, meaningful, and thriving relationships. 224 pages, hardcover.

SA192575   Retail $23.00   . . . . **$16.49**

Foundations
Troy Simons

You want your kids to become disciples, but where do you begin? Ruth and Troy Simons explore 12 truths that will help you connect your children's hearts to God. 192 pages, hardcover.

SA969109   Retail $22.99   . . . . **$14.99**

The Power of Being Thankful
Joyce Meyer

Discover the power of a grateful heart! This 365-day devotional is designed to spark an attitude of gratitude and features inspiring readings, Scripture verses, and prayers of thanks. 384 pages, hardcover.

SA517336   Retail $17.00   . . . . **$10.49**

Seeing Jesus from the East
Ravi Zacharias & Abdu Murray

Presenting a broader view of Christ, the authors uncover aspects of the gospel often overlooked by Westerners as they explore the themes of honor, sacrifice, and more through an Eastern lens. 256 pages, hardcover.

SA531289   Retail $26.99   . . . . **$17.99**

Experiencing Israel
Tony Evans

Make your faith journey come alive! Evans offers an up-close look at the Holy Land through stunning color photos, vivid descriptions, and practical applications of God's Word. 144 pages, hardcover.

SA975662   Retail $29.99   . . . . **$17.99**

SAVE 40%

Fervent
Priscilla Shirer

SAVE 41%

Satan wants to personally destroy you! Fight back with the most effective weapon—prayer. Shirer shows you how to renew your passion, deal with regrets, uproot bitterness, and more. 208 pages, softcover.

SA688676   Retail $16.99   . . . . **$9.99**

Planted with a Purpose
T.D. Jakes

If God is all-powerful, why does he allow suffering? Wrestling with this age-old question, Jakes concludes the Lord uses difficult experiences to prepare us for unexpected blessings. 128 pages, hardcover.

SA017813   Retail $10.00   . . . . **$7.99**

Fundamentals of the Faith
John MacArthur

Blending biblical truths with personal obedience and service, this 13-lesson discipleship curriculum discusses topics ranging from an introduction to Scripture to the attributes of God. 112 pages, softcover.

10 or more $6.49 each

SA438393   Retail $11.99   . . . . **$6.99**

ENDORSEMENTS

If you've ever wanted a deeper relationship with God, this is the book for you. Backed by scripture and practical steps, Karen helps you understand clearly just how much God loves you and wants to be close to you. I highly recommend this book.

—Lynne Hammond
Living Word Christian Center
Brooklyn Park, Minnesota
Author of *The Master is Calling*
lynnehammond.org

The closer we get to our Heavenly Father, the more the Holy Spirit can work in us to accomplish God's purpose in us. Karen's purpose in this book is to help you get as close as you desire. I believe it can help you in your own life, then empower you to reach out and bless others.

—Dr. Pat Harrison
Founder Faith Christian Fellowship International
Author of *Overflowing With the Holy Spirit*
patharrisonministries.com

I am happy to recommend another great book by my friend, Karen Jensen Salisbury! No matter how well you know God, this book, with it's easy-to-understand biblical truths, can help you get even closer to Him. Karen writes to her readers with an open and engaging style—this book can change your relationship with God and change your life!

—BETH JONES
Pastor Valley Family Church, Kalamazoo, Michigan
Author of *The Basics with Beth*
thebasicswithbeth.com

Our personal ambition, above all, is to know God more every day. We can think of no higher purpose for any believer's life. That is why we're excited about Karen Jensen Salisbury's latest book. Writing from the perspective of her own authentic relationship with the Lord, Karen provides practical and easy-to-understand guidance that leaves the reader inspired and equipped to have the relationship with God we've always dreamed possible.

—MATT & JULIE BEEMER
Missionaries to the Middle East
International Directors of CLUB1040.com

I'm pleased to recommend another book by Karen Jensen Salisbury. If you want to get closer to God, you'll love this book.

—SANDY SCHEER
Co-Pastor Guts Church, Tulsa, Oklahoma
gutschurch.com

My father and I are proud to have Karen Jensen Salisbury as one of our talk show hosts on the *Oasis Radio Network*; and we're also proud of her literary accomplishments, including this newest book. Karen's writing style is similar to her interviews—engaging, encouraging, and inspiring. Let Karen help you go from "close" to "closer" in your relationship with God.

—David Warren Ingles
Program Director, *Oasis Radio Network*
oasisnetwork.org

Another fantastic book! Whenever Karen Jensen Salisbury writes a book, it's worth reading, and this one is no exception—it can answer the cry of your heart to having a closer, more intimate, more powerful relationship with God, which is priceless. This is a must-read book.

—Tim & Renee Burt
TimBurt.org

Karen Jensen Salisbury is an amazing teacher and writer. We have known her for years and are so impressed with her passion for God and to get the message of love, truth and encouragement out to the body of Christ. This book will encourage your walk with God and show you how to draw close to him through developing your relationship with Him, so you can feel His presence, hear His voice, and receive His guidance every day. We highly recommend this new book.

—Rod & Rebecca Sundholm
Pastors, New Creation Church, Hillsboro, Oregon
nccoregon.com

HARRISON HOUSE BOOKS BY
KAREN JENSEN SALISBURY

I Forgive You But…

Closer Than You Ever Imagined

EXPERIENCING THE DEEP RELATIONSHIP WITH GOD YOU ALWAYS WANTED

Karen Jensen Salisbury

Published by Harrison House Publishers
Shippensburg, PA 17257

Cover design by Eileen Rockwell
Interior design by Terry Clifton

ISBN 13 TP: 978-1-6803-1413-7
ISBN 13 eBook: 978-1-6803-1419-9
ISBN 13 HC: 978-1-6803-1438-0
ISBN 13 LP: 978-1-6803-1437-3

For Worldwide Distribution, Printed in the U.S.A.

1 2 3 4 5 6 7 8 / 24 23 22 21 20

CONTENTS

INTRODUCTION

EVERYWHERE I GO PEOPLE SAY TO ME, "KAREN, I WANT WHAT you have—I want be close to God like you are." I usually tell them, "If you're a Christian, you already *have* what I have!" But obviously, they don't know it, or they don't know how to get closer to God than they are.

The good news is that you can always get closer to God! He wants you to. He's ready and willing and able to have the most intimate relationship possible with you.

Let me be clear: even though I'm writing a book about getting closer to God, it doesn't mean that I have the closest relationship with Him on the planet. I don't by any means know all there is to know.

Nobody does! God is so deep! No one knows everything about Him—the depth of His greatness is beyond measurement. Psalm 145:3 says that no one can fathom His greatness (NIV). God is *fathomless!* The definition of *fathomless* is "to be too deep to be measured; to be bottomless."

You and I will spend all eternity getting to know Him more, getting closer and closer to Him.

But we *can* know Him better tomorrow than we do today. We can go deeper in our relationship with Him and get closer to Him every day. That's my goal every day—to get closer to Him.

> # We can know Him better tomorrow than we do today. He wants us to!

We'll never get all the way to "perfect knowledge of God" or the pinnacle of closeness with Him. He's fathomless, remember? There will always be more of Him to know and get closer to.

But you *can* get closer to God. Every day! I want to give you information and help you with some practical steps. Thus, this book. God loves you! You are the apple of His eye! He created you for His pleasure! And amazingly enough, He wants to be closer to you, too. Christianity is not a religion; it is a relationship.

He Wanted to Be Closer

Think about it: in the Old Testament, God's presence on earth lived in a box—the Ark of the Covenant. He commanded that the Ark be placed in the center of the Israelites' life—first in the Tabernacle that was placed at the center of their camp as they traveled through the wilderness to the Promised Land, and later in the Temple that was in the center of the city.

Even under the Old Covenant, our God wasn't a far-away God—He was a right-up-close God. He wanted to live right in the center of His people.

> **Even under the Old Covenant, our God wasn't a far-away God— He was a right-up-close God.**

But even that wasn't close enough for Him. In Jeremiah 31 He said, *"Behold, the days are coming, says the Lord, when I will make a new covenant with the house of Israel and with the house of Judah…I will put My law in their minds, and write it on their hearts; and I will be their God, and they shall be My people"* (Jer. 31:31,33). In Ezekiel 36:26 He said, *"I will give you a new heart and put a new spirit within you."*

In other words, God wanted to be even closer to His people—He wanted to live in us. And that's just what He did, through Jesus Christ. And Jesus Himself promised, *"I will pray the Father, and He will give you another Helper, that He may abide with you forever—the Spirit of truth, whom the world cannot receive, because it neither sees Him nor knows Him; but you know Him, for He dwells with you and will be in you"* (John 14:16-17).

And that's exactly what happened. The Bible says that *your body* is now the temple of the Holy Spirit! (See 1 Corinthians 6:19.) He doesn't live in a box anymore—He lives in you! You can't get any closer than that. That's how close He wants to be to us.

I think that's so amazing! Of all the religions in the world, only one God lives inside His people. That's how close He wants to be to you. He wants to be known by you! We don't have a relationship with a religion or even with the Bible—we have a relationship with Him. He is our loving Father.

The Creator of heaven and earth, Almighty God, ruler of the universe, wants to be in you and known by you. That just thrills my heart every day, and I hope it thrills your heart too. When you know Him, it's always fresh, never boring. It makes me want to be closer and closer to Him every day.

Those Who Know Their God

The book of Daniel tells us, *"the people who know their God shall be strong, and carry out great exploits"* (Dan. 11:32). The Merriam-Webster dictionary defines an *exploit* as "a

notable or heroic act." I get excited about carrying out notable or heroic acts for God, don't you?

Notice it doesn't say that the people who are super spiritual or strong in themselves will do great exploits. No, it's
the people who *know their God*. Apparently, we can get
close enough to God to know Him and to do notable and
heroic acts by Him. That sounds like good news to me.

**We can get close enough to God
to know Him and to do notable
and heroic acts for Him.**

And Daniel knew what he was talking about. He
was just a young man when he and the Israelites were
taken captive from their homeland to the heathen nation
of Babylon and forced to assimilate to a foreign culture.
When he and his friends risked their lives by standing up
to the king and refusing to eat food that God had out-
lawed, they ended up looking healthier than anyone else,
and they were granted more wisdom than anyone in the
kingdom (see Dan. 1:1-20).

When they refused to bow down to an idol and were
thrown into a fiery furnace as a result, God rescued

them and they didn't even smell like smoke afterward (see Dan. 3:8-27)! In his later life, when Daniel refused to stop praying to God three times a day and was thrown into a den of man-eating lions, God sent His angel and shut the lions' mouths so that Daniel was completely unharmed (see Dan. 6:1-28).

All of these notable and heroic acts happened because Daniel knew his God. All through the book of Daniel we see him praying and obeying. He showed us a life of closeness to God, consecrated to knowing Him, and the results were great exploits!

I say, let's get closer and closer to God—let's get to know Him better and better and do some great exploits of our own that bring Him glory and set people free.

We Have It Even Better

As awesome as Daniel was in doing great exploits, he was an old covenant child of God. You and I are *new covenant* children of God, and according to Hebrews 8:6 we have an even better covenant based on even better promises! Do you suppose that means we can do even *greater* exploits than Daniel did? Jesus said we could in John 14:12:

> *Most assuredly, I say to you, he who believes in Me, the works that I do he will do also; and greater works than these he will do, because I go to My Father.*

In the New Testament, the apostle Paul said, *"[my determined purpose is] that I may know Him"* (Phil. 3:10 AMPC).

Now, think about this. Paul didn't say that his determined purpose was to reach most of the known world with the Gospel...although he did that. He didn't say that his determined purpose was to write half the New Testament... although he did that too. He didn't say that his determined purpose was to perform miracles in the name of Jesus... even though he did that too!

No, his determined purpose was to know God—to get closer and closer to the Father, and *because of that* he did all those other things. His main focus was getting closer to God—and the result was reaching the world with the Gospel, writing half the New Testament, and performing miracles in Jesus' Name.

What might happen in *your* life and sphere of influence if your determined purpose was to know God?

This book is about that. Can we get closer to Him? Can we know Him better? I think we can—I think we're supposed to. He is ready, willing, and able to have the closest relationship possible with you, if you want it. He wants to be known!

God's Not Hiding from You

Sometimes we can feel like God is far away from us, not answering us when we call. But we can't go by feelings. He is very close to us! The Bible even calls Jesus *Immanuel*— which means "God with us" (Matt. 1:23). He's not God far away from us or hiding from us—He's God *with* us!

God is ready, willing, and able to have the closest relationship possible with you, if you want it.

Our heavenly Father is an open book, if we choose to read Him. After Paul stated in the first part of Philippians 3:10 that his determined purpose was to know God, he continued the thought: *"[that I may progressively become more deeply and intimately acquainted with Him, perceiving and recognizing and understanding the wonders of His Person more strongly and more clearly]"* (AMPC).

We can do that too. God wants us to.

There's a difference between knowing *about* someone and knowing them. You and I know *about* our favorite movie star or political figure—we know who they're married to, where they live, maybe what they like to eat or what their favorite color is. But we don't have their personal cell number or know their true motivations and desires. We've probably never even met them in person. We don't really *know* them like we do someone who is close to us.

Lots of people are like that with God. They know some things *about* Him, but they don't really *know* Him. They don't know what to expect from Him in a given situation because they're not intimately acquainted with Him.

It takes time to truly know someone. And it takes proximity—you have to be in the same place at the same time, sharing things, going through some things together so that you know what to expect from each other when real-life pressures come along. Paul had that with God. And that's the kind of deeper relationship God wants with you, too. He wants to be closer than you've ever imagined.

Are you ready to get closer to God? To have His power and glory and love flowing freely through your life? Let's go....

Chapter 1

HOW I GOT CLOSER TO GOD

ON NEW YEAR'S DAY 1997, MY HUSBAND, BRENT, WENT TO bed before me. We'd been up late the night before at a New Year's Eve party at the church we pastored, and while I'd had time for a nap during that day, he had not.

At about 8:30 P.M., he bent over the couch where I was sitting, gave me a quick kiss, and said, "Night! I love you." I smiled and said, "I love you back." And he headed off to bed.

That was last time I saw him alive.

When I got to the bedroom a couple hours later, he wasn't breathing. I called 911 and the paramedics came, but he was never revived. He hadn't been sick or anything—he just went to bed and went to heaven at 37 years of age. (You can read more about it in my book *Why God Why: What to Do When Life Doesn't Make Sense.*)

As you can imagine, that event rocked my world. I was caught completely by surprise. Our sons were 12 and 13 years old, and the three of us were plunged into a season of grief and bewilderment. As for me, I had to take over parenting teenage sons, pastoring our four-and-a-half-year-old church, and getting over the sudden death of my husband.

I Fell in Love

That was over 20 years ago now, and looking back I can see that while it was the worst time of my life, you could say it was also the best time of my life. I know that sounds weird, but it's true. Because I pressed into God like never before, and He met me in a profound and life-changing way. He was right there, a very present help, drawing near to me every time I drew near to Him. It's really the time I fell in love with Him.

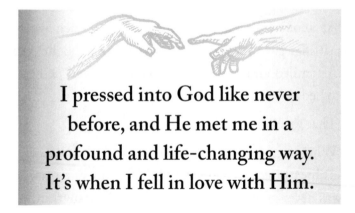

I pressed into God like never before, and He met me in a profound and life-changing way. It's when I fell in love with Him.

At the time, people said to me, "You're being so brave, staying with God through all this. I might be mad at Him!"

Well, I may not be the brightest bulb in the box, but I knew that it was no time to get mad at God and walk away from Him—not when I needed Him most! I had to raise teenage boys, pastor a church, and get past grief—I needed all the help I could get. And I knew God was the answer.

So I pressed into Him like never before. I spent hours reading my Bible. I would run my finger down the page like a five-year-old learning how to read. I *absorbed* it. I was desperate for His peace, His comfort, His guidance—I *had to have it*—and I knew His Word was the place to find it. God's Word is Him talking to us, and I wanted to hear Him every minute during those first days of recovery.

Psalm 119:92-93 says it like this, *"Unless Your law had been my delight, I would then have perished in my affliction. I will never forget Your precepts, for by them You have given me life."* That was me. I was in a time of trouble and affliction, but His Word was a lifeline for me—I felt like I would have perished without it. Night after night I just sat in a quiet place and let His Word wash over me. He gave me life through His Word—it was my delight.

There is something to that idea of being delighted by spending time with God. Psalm 37:4 says, *"Delight yourself also in the Lord, and He shall give you the desires of your heart."* His Word was my delight, and as a result He gave me the desires of my heart.

I discovered later that these times spent with God were a delight to His heart as well as mine. He loves spending time with His children.

Now, I'm not saying that you have to read the Bible for hours and hours to get to know God. You don't "earn and deserve" a relationship with God—He already took care of all that in Jesus (we'll talk more about that in the next chapter). But the Bible is God talking to us. It contains His instructions, His character, His promises, His hopes and dreams for mankind—and for you. It's the first place to go when you want to get closer to Him.

> ## The Bible is God talking to us. It's the first place to go when you want to get closer to Him.

I found Him through His Word. I found out He is so faithful, so available for us whenever we call upon Him. Psalm 46:1 says, *"God is our refuge and strength, a very present help in trouble."* I found out firsthand that's absolutely true! As I drew nearer and nearer to Him, He was such a *present* help—I could feel Him right there with me each day as I navigated my way through the days and months after my husband's death.

James 4:8 says, *"Draw near to God and He will draw near to you."* He is true to this promise—He is always available for you when you draw near to Him. There's really no one else you can say that about. Think about it: even the people you love most can't be available for you 24/7. There are times you might call on them and get their voice mail, or they're simply too busy to drop everything and rush to your aid.

But not your Father God. He's never too busy for you. You'll never get His voice mail. *Every single time* you draw near to Him, He'll draw near to you.

Now, I would say that I knew God before my husband died. I would even say I loved Him, yes! I had read all those verses before. I had preached the Word and been a faith girl. But there's something about pressing in during a time of need—a time of desperation, really—that helped me find out that He really is a very present help in times of trouble. That time period after my husband died is really when I fell in love with God.

Why? Because I spent so much time with Him.

Only One Thing Is Needed

My story reminds me of a story in the Bible. I got so much closer to God when I spent time with Him—when I chose to sit at His feet, much like a woman named Mary chose to sit at Jesus' feet when He came to her house one day.

Her story is in Luke 10:38-42, where one day Jesus paid a visit to the house she shared with her brother Lazarus and her sister Martha. Jesus probably brought quite a few people with Him, as He rarely traveled alone, and He also probably didn't call ahead for reservations. So that meant that Mary and Martha had quite a bit of work to do to serve a meal to all those people at a moment's notice.

It was obviously pretty stressful, because we see Martha in the kitchen, plucking the chickens, preparing the salad, making the lemonade, ordering the servants around, banging the pots and pans—and then suddenly she looked around her and noticing that *Mary was not in there helping.*

We know this ticked Martha off, because she immediately ran into her living room and *yelled at the Lord* (you know you're pretty stressed out when you yell at the Lord in your living room).

With the vein standing out in her neck, Martha sputtered, "Lord, I'm working pretty hard in here! Make my sister help me!" I'm sure she totally expected Jesus to say, "Oh, you poor girl, yes! Mary, go help your sister." But no. Instead Jesus focused on Martha with a look of compassion and said, *"Martha, Martha, you are worried and troubled about many things. But one thing is needed, and Mary has chosen that good part, which will not be taken away from her"* (Luke 10:41-42).

In her frenzy, Martha thought that 65 things were needed to get dinner on the table that day. She thought someone needed to roast the chicken, mash the potatoes, pour the drinks, set the table, etc. But Jesus said that *only one thing* was needed, and Mary was doing it.

What was Mary doing? She was sitting at the feet of Jesus. Spending time with Him. Listening to Him.

Jesus was obviously trying to tell Martha to stop working so hard and getting so agitated. He wanted her to know that spending time with Him is more beneficial than stressing over all the things *she* thought needed to get done. And what Mary garnered from that time with Him could never be taken away from her. She benefitted in ways that would last a lifetime. Wow!

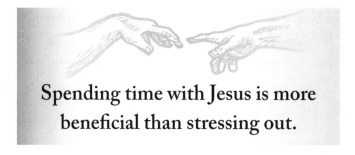

Spending time with Jesus is more beneficial than stressing out.

We don't get to see what happened after Jesus said that to Martha. It was probably one of two things—she either huffed away, even madder than before, or she let His words sink into her heart and just stopped the merry-go-round right then and there, sinking to His feet to listen. I hope that's what she did!

Because if she did, all sorts of miracles might have happened. Think about this: just one chapter before, Jesus had miraculously turned a few loaves and fish into a meal for 5,000 people (see Luke 9:10-17). I don't think He would have had any trouble getting a meal on the table at Mary and Martha's house. Could Martha's attempt to do everything in her own strength have stopped a miracle from happening at her house that day?

I think that quick little Bible story is such a powerful illustration of time spent with Jesus. Putting Him first, sitting at His feet, reading His words, listening for His voice does us so much good! That's what I did after my husband died, and it changed everything for me.

Spending time with Him is how we get closer and closer to Him—how we get to know Him better and better. It's how we avail ourselves of miracles; how we put ourselves in a position of peace and rest so we can clearly hear His perfect guidance for our life.

> **Putting Him first, sitting at His feet, reading His words, listening to His voice does us so much good!**

And I believe it also shows how we trust Him. When we say, "Lord, I'm setting aside all the pressing things that need to be done right now and making *You* my priority," don't you think that brings joy to His heart and gets Him excited about working miracles in your life? If someone says that to you—"I'm making *you* my priority right now instead of all this other important stuff"—doesn't it make you feel wonderful and feel like helping them? It makes you feel even more in love with them. The same thing happens when we choose to spend more time with God.

Who Moved?

I want you to notice, though, that God leaves it up to us. He's always available, but He's waiting for us to draw near. He's not going to come rudely barreling into our life, telling us what to do or how He can help—He's a gentleman. It's up to *us* how much time we spend—in His Word, in prayer, in meditating. It's up to us how close we want to get. Isn't that marvelous? We get to decide how close we want to be to God!

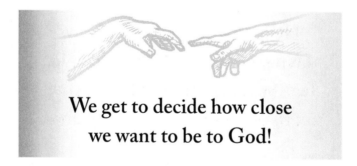

We get to decide how close we want to be to God!

It reminds me of a story. Once upon a time, a young man was dating a young woman. If you happened to be driving behind his pick-up truck when the two of them were on a date, you'd see the young lady sitting so close to her beloved on the bench seat that from your car behind they almost looked like one person.

Fast-forward several years—the two got married, had a couple of children, and now if you drive behind them, you'd see her sitting over on the passenger side of the pick-up next to the door and him sitting behind the wheel. One day she looks over at her husband and says, "Honey, I feel like we've grown apart."

Her husband looks at her, then looks at the steering wheel—looks at her again and looks at the steering wheel again. Finally he says, "Who moved?"

He is always available, always loving you, always ready to help, always ready to draw near.

It's like that in your relationship with God. He is always the same—He never moves. He is always available, always loving you, always ready to help, always ready to draw near. You are the one who moved away. Most of the time it happens gradually—like it probably did for that young couple. You get busy with life and other things take up your attention and time.

But one day you look around and realize that you're not as close to God as you used to be or you want to be. He's still in the same place, waiting for you, but you've scooted away. The good news is, you can scoot back! He's not mad or even resentful toward you—He won't say, "What took you so long?" or cast any disparaging looks at you. No, He's waiting with open arms to welcome you back to the closeness! Or maybe to welcome you to that kind of closeness for the first time.

You Can Trust Him

I know there are some who don't want to be any closer to God than they already are. They're afraid of that much intimacy, of baring their soul to someone, letting them see all the good, the bad, and the ugly inside. Because chances are that they've been hurt, and they have trouble trusting.

But I want you to know that you can trust God. He's not like other people who have let you down or made fun of you. He's your heavenly Father and He loves you unconditionally (we'll talk more about that in Chapter 4). You must understand how trustworthy God is if you want to become closer to Him. You don't have to hold Him at arm's length. You can trust Him.

I've heard of people who don't want a relationship with God—or don't want to spend time listening to Him—because they think He'll ask them to do something hard or do something they don't want to do. Maybe you've heard it too—something like: "If I turn my life over to God, He might make me be a missionary to Africa, and I don't want to go!"

But here's the deal: God doesn't *make* us do anything. In Jeremiah 29:11 He says, *"I know the plans I have for you… plans to prosper you and not to harm you, plans to give you hope and a future"* (NIV). God has a plan for your life, and it's a *good* plan. It's not a bad plan! It's a plan that uses all your passions, all your giftings—a plan that will make you happier than you ever imagined. There's nothing better than walking in God's plan for your life.

There's nothing better than walking in God's plan for your life.

But He's not going to *make* you do the plan. He is going to anoint you and give you giftings and personality traits that make you perfect for the plan, and He will prompt you and do His best to guide you into it, but He will always leave it up to you.

Any time He asks you to do *anything*, it's only for your good. You are not His puppet, someone to be pulled and prodded to do His bidding at a whim—you are His beloved child, and He wants only the best for you. He's not like other people, who may have their own agenda for your life. His only agenda is to bless you. Period.

Proverbs 3:5-6 says, *"Trust in the Lord with all your heart, and lean not on your own understanding. In all your ways acknowledge Him, and He shall direct your paths."* God knows so much more than we do. He sees the end beginning from the beginning (see Isa. 46:10)! When we trust Him, it gives Him free reign to guide our lives.

Trusting the Lord simply means believing Him. It means you read His promises in the Bible and simply take Him at His word—you just believe what He's said.

We do this all the time in the natural realm. When we send money to an online store, we believe that they'll keep their word and send us the item we paid for, even before we see it. We trust the store. God is so much more trustworthy!

For one thing, He always keeps His Word. Paul said it this way in Second Corinthians 1:20: *"For all the promises of God in Him are Yes, and in Him Amen, to the glory of God through us."* His promises are all true, and He will bring them to pass.

God is not like other people you may have known in your life—people you couldn't depend on. You can depend on Him! He always tells the truth. All His promises are "yes! And so be it!"

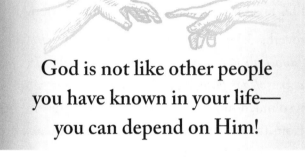

God is not like other people you have known in your life— you can depend on Him!

He is your loving heavenly Father. Hebrews 11:6 says that He is a rewarder of those who diligently seek Him. But you must believe that. He is so pleased when you draw near to Him in faith—He wants you to believe Him! That verse also says that *without faith it is impossible to please Him*—we must believe that He is, and that He is a rewarder.

God knows that other people may have hurt you and as a result you may struggle with the fact that He is good and wants to shower you with His goodness. So many of us resist God and don't trust in His goodness because we don't know who He is and what He has given us in Christ.

But you can know Him! And you can trust Him. He doesn't want you to feel guilty or angry, as some religious teaching may have told you. He's not mad at you: He's madly in love with you! Jeremiah 31:3 says, *"I have loved you with an everlasting love; therefore with lovingkindness I have drawn you."*

It's funny—plenty of people believe there *is* a God— they just don't believe in His goodness. They don't believe that He loves them. In fact, they often believe that He's mad or irritated at them. It just seems too good to be true that the Creator of the universe loves them unconditionally. They just aren't convinced that God is good and He is love (see 1 John 4:8).

But it's true, and His only agenda toward you is for good, not for evil.

What About the Bad Stuff?

Some people are confused about what comes from God and what comes from the devil. Maybe you've heard someone say, "If God is so good, why does so much bad stuff happen?" They think God is responsible for the evil things that take place in the world. In fact, insurance companies call things like hurricanes, tornados and earthquakes "acts of God." Wrong!

John 10:10 clearly shows us what comes from God and what comes from the devil. Jesus said, *"The thief does not come except to steal, and to kill, and to destroy. I have come that they may have life, and that they may have it more abundantly."* So here's how you tell what comes from God and what comes from the devil—if there is any killing, stealing, or destroying going on, it was the devil, not God!

You can't trust someone if you think they are causing or allowing the pain, destruction, or loss in your life. You must settle it in your heart, once and for all, that God is *good*, He has a good plan for you, He loves you, and you can trust Him.

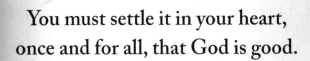

You must settle it in your heart, once and for all, that God is good.

God knows that it's hard for humans to trust some-one they can't see or someone they've only heard bad things about all their lives. But He wants you to know you can depend on Him. There are a lot of scriptures in the Bible that say the Lord is good; here are just a few:

> *Oh, taste and see that the Lord is good; blessed is the man who trusts in Him!* (Psalm 34:8)
>
> *For the Lord is good; His mercy is everlasting, and His truth endures to all generations* (Psalm 100:5).
>
> *Praise the Lord, for the Lord is good; sing praises to His name, for it is pleasant* (Psalm 135:3).
>
> *The Lord is good to all, and His tender mercies are over all His works* (Psalm 145:9).
>
> *Praise the Lord of hosts, for the Lord is good, for His mercy endures forever* (Jeremiah 33:11).
>
> *The Lord is good to those who wait for Him, to the soul who seeks Him* (Lamentations 3:25).

The Lord is good, a stronghold in the day of trouble; and He knows those who trust in Him (Nahum 1:7).

That phrase is in the Bible over and over because it's *true*—He is good. And when you begin to know and understand that truth, then you can trust Him with all your heart. God is good to us every day, all day. We can trust Him.

What does it mean to write these truths on the tablet of your heart? It simply means to meditate and think about them. Every time you have the thought that God isn't helping, or He is mad, or He's causing your problems, instead switch over to thinking about His goodness and all He has promised in His Word. Think about how much He loves you!

When you do that, your heart will begin to believe that you can trust God. It will become persuaded and established in this truth. When that happens, then your emotions will begin to fall in line—you'll actually begin to *feel* like you can trust Him. Remember, feelings follow *after* faith.

I promise you, this will dramatically change how you see yourself and how you see and interact with God. It will even help your relationships, because you'll be undergirded with the greatest love of all—you won't be needy or fearful or clingy in your relationships because you'll be secure in God's love for you. Best of all, it will change how you see

God. You'll be able to trust Him because you'll see love and mercy toward you.

When you trust the Lord, you'll be able to experience perfect peace. There's nothing like it! In situations where you used to feel stressed or worried or fearful or confused, now you'll have peace—a certain knowing in your heart that God is with you and taking care of you. You won't be leaning to *your* understanding; you'll be trusting Him.

God isn't saying that we don't have any understanding. Trusting Him simply means that we know He has a better way than we do. When you trust Him, He'll show you how to handle things in life that you need His wisdom for.

When you trust Him, He'll show you how to handle things in life that you need His wisdom for.

Another wonderful benefit of trusting God completely is that He will direct your path—He will guide you every day. He will be in charge of your comings and goings, make sure you're in the right place at the right time. That has huge implications for your life.

Every morning of my life I pray, "Father, put me in the right place at the right time, with the right people doing the right thing. Make me a blessing!" When I fully trust God to do that, I am always doing the right thing! I'm always in position to overcome, to be there to help someone at just the right moment, to not waste time but make the most of all my time.

How I Came to Trust Him

I learned to trust God during that time after my first husband died. I thought I trusted Him before, but that was the time when the rubber really met the road, and I found Him to be completely trustworthy.

I had agreed to take over the pastorate of the church, but in the weeks that followed my husband's death I didn't preach every service right at first. I just wasn't ready yet—I needed some time to recover and to ease into the office of pastor. So in my place, I had guest minister friends who came to help preach the services.

Inevitably after one of them preached, they'd want to pray for people, and specifically they'd want to pray for me. So at the end of each service, the visiting minster would have an altar call, pray for people, and then pray for me. As a result, I would usually end up sitting in the sanctuary for quite a while afterward, basking in the presence of God long after everyone else went home.

God ministered so sweetly to my heart during those times of basking in His presence. And the first few times, as I sat there in the quiet, I would eventually say to Him, "Father, as long as we're here together, and You're healing my heart and mind so wonderfully, is there anything You'd like to tell me about *what in the world happened?*" I had so many questions as to why my healthy, vital 37-year-old husband just went to bed and went to heaven.

And God's answer was always the same. He said, "Can you trust Me?" Well, I knew it was no time to stop trusting Him, when I had to get past grief, pastor the church, and raise the sons by myself. And what are you going to say to God anyway when He asks you a question like that point blank? "No"? Of course not. So I always answered, "Yes, Lord, I trust You."

"Can you trust Me?"

It only took about seven or eight times for me to finally understand what God was trying to get through to me. He was trying to tell me that I might not get all the answers I wanted, but that He would lead, guide, direct, and help me every step of the way for the rest of my life if I believed Him and kept trusting Him.

So after about the eighth time that God asked me if I could trust Him, I finally said, "Okay, okay! I get it. This is Your answer. So yes, Father—I can trust You. I *will* trust You. I won't ask again."

It was a pivotal moment in our relationship. I felt the shift. When I chose to trust Him fully, even though I still had questions and I didn't like the situation, I felt closer to Him than ever before. And in the next 17 years, I watched Him do miracles in my life and the lives of my sons. They got to attend a Christian university, I got the job of my dreams, got to travel and preach around the world, and then I got remarried to a wonderful, godly man.

I discovered that our heavenly Father just wants us to believe Him. As we do, He'll give us the desires of our heart—and then some (see Ps. 37:4)! He's not asking us for the impossible—He's not asking us to do things in our own strength. He's asking us to trust and believe Him. We can do that!

Review in a Nutshell

God wants to be closer to you, and the way to do that is through His Word and spending time with Him. You can trust Him! He has no other agenda but *good* for your life.

Now Engage:

Read and meditate the scriptures we've looked at, and activate the power of God's Word in your life by speaking these declarations out loud.

> *Unless Your law had been my delight, I would then have perished in my affliction. I will never forget Your precepts, for by them You have given me life* (Psalm 119:92-93).

Declare:

> "I delight in reading God's Word, because I know it's God talking to me. Whenever I'm in trouble, I will go to the Bible—without it I would perish. I need it in my life every day! God's Word gives me life."

> *Delight yourself also in the Lord, and He shall give you the desires of your heart* (Psalm 37:4).

Declare:

> "I am delighted to spend time in God's Word, getting to know Him better and better, and I know that He is giving me the desires of my

heart. I love spending time with God, and I know He loves spending time with me!"

God is our refuge and strength, a very present help in trouble (Psalm 46:1).

Declare:

"I'm so thankful that in times of trouble, God is with me! He isn't far away from me—He's right up close, helping me, rescuing me, being my refuge and strength."

Draw near to God and He will draw near to you (James 4:8).

Declare:

"Every time I draw near to God, He draws near to me. There's never a time I'll get His voice mail or a busy signal—He always has time for me. Even my closest family and friends aren't as available to me as my Father God is."

Martha, Martha, you are worried and troubled about many things. But one thing is needed, and Mary has chosen that good part, which will not be taken away from her (Luke 10:41-42).

Declare:

"When I'm tempted to worry or be over-whelmed when a lot is going on, I'll stop the crazy cycle and choose to spend time in the presence of the Lord. When it looks like a hundred things need to happen, I will do the *one* thing that is needed—I will spend time with God and get His wisdom, help, and insight."

I know the plans I have for you...plans to prosper you and not to harm you, plans to give you hope and a future (Jeremiah 29:11 NIV).

Declare:

"God has a plan for my life, and it's a *good* plan! It's a plan that uses all my passions and giftings—a plan that will make me happier than I ever imagined. I choose to walk in it. I trust Him."

Trust in the Lord with all your heart, and lean not on your own understanding. In all your ways acknowledge Him, and He shall direct your paths (Proverbs 3:5-6).

Declare:

"God knows more than I do. I trust Him—I give Him free reign to guide my life. I believe what He has said in His Word."

For all the promises of God in Him are Yes, and in Him Amen, to the glory of God through us (2 Corinthians 1:20).

Declare:

> "God's promises are all true, and He will bring them to pass. He's not like other people I've known whom I couldn't depend on. I can depend on Him! He always tells the truth and keeps His promises."

I have loved you with an everlasting love; therefore with lovingkindness I have drawn you (Jeremiah 31:3).

Declare:

> "I can know God better and better, and I can trust Him. He doesn't want me to feel guilty or angry. He's not mad at me—He's madly in love with me! I believe in His goodness and His love."

The thief does not come except to steal, and to kill, and to destroy. I have come that they may have life, and that they may have it more abundantly (John 10:10).

Declare:

> "I know that if there is any killing, stealing, or destroying going on, it was the devil, not God! God is good, and Jesus came to give us abundant life. I won't get confused about what is caused by God and what is caused by the devil."

For the Lord is good; His mercy is everlasting, and His truth endures to all generations (Psalm 100:5).

Declare:

"I am understanding more every day that God is *good*. I settle it in my heart, once and for all, that He is good, He has a good plan for me, He loves me, and I can trust Him."

Discussion Questions:

How well would you say you know God? Do you want to know Him more? After reading this chapter, do you feel like it's possible? Have you had trouble trusting God? If so, why?

Chapter Two

What God Did to Bring You Closer

From the very beginning of Creation, God wanted fellowship. It's why He created us. He wanted a family.

That's the opposite of the way the world portrays Him. Many people believe that God exists, but they think of Him as sitting on His throne far away in heaven, looking down on humans with distaste, disinterest, or irritation. They say things like, "God's going to get you!" and think He's sitting up there with a big baseball bat, ready to bop anyone who doesn't do things His way.

Or they think of Him as ruling the universe, way too busy to be interested or involved in their lives.

Nothing could be further from the truth! God loves us! From the very beginning of the Bible, we see Him creating heaven and earth in the book of Genesis, and He made it all for us. He lovingly created the earth for mankind, His crowning glory (see Ps. 8:4-6). He created it all for someone

He could love and fellowship with. He prepared the earth for His creation just as a parent prepares a nursery for their much-loved, much-anticipated baby.

God created you and me for fellowship. He wanted a family.

Made in His Image

When the earth was all finished and ready, God created man in His own image (see Gen. 1:27). He made man because He wanted another being whom He could fellowship with on an equal plane. He formed Adam out of the dust and then He breathed His very life into him (see Gen. 2:7).

Imagine that. There was Adam—a being as pure and holy as God Himself, with God's life in him. He had all the same attributes as God did. And God had someone He could share His heart and His power with. He had a true son.

As beautiful as nature is on planet Earth—the mountains, the oceans, the trees, the rivers, the deserts, the sky—it was not made in His image the way we are. God considers *us* His masterpiece (see Eph. 2:10 NLT), and we need to see ourselves that way too. He made all that *for* us. None of God's other creations—animals, birds, fish—could stand face to face with God like man could. In the Garden of Eden, God walked with Adam and Eve face to face every day, in the cool of the evening (see Gen. 3:8).

It was always God's idea to be close to us. Fellowship and closeness with us was His greatest dream. He wanted that kind of communion and that kind of communication with us. He gave mankind dominion over the earth (see Gen. 1:26), not because He needed the help (He wasn't looking for employees!) but because He was placing mankind on His level. He is a God who rules and reigns, and He gave that kind of authority to His created man. It's something God and mankind have in common.

Of course, fellowship happens more readily between people who have things in common, especially shared responsibilities. For example, policemen like to fellowship with other policemen, because they understand each other in a way that non-cops don't. They "get it." They have things in common. God wanted someone who "gets it" in fellowship with Him.

I have friends who are nurses, and when they get together in conversation, I'm sort of left out of the loop because they have a shared interest and shared responsibilities. They can all tell stories of emergency surgeries and difficult patients and miracle medical procedures, and I can't. They "get it" when it comes to working in the medical field, and as a result, they have a bond that I can't share with them. We all love each other, but their fellowship has an added element that brings them closer.

It's like that with God. He made us to fellowship with, so He originally gave us the same power, dominion, and authority in the earth that He had so we would have that in common with Him. He wanted a family—not just to take care of, but a family of sons and daughters who would grow up and share His dominion with Him and love Him because they understood. That's what creating the earth was all about.

Man Has a Free Will

God created everything mankind needed for a wonderful, fruitful, abundant life to live forever in the beautiful Garden. He created man with fellowship, communion, and a sharing of hearts in mind. That was God's initial covenant with Adam and Eve.

He only asked one thing for their part in the covenant—don't eat the fruit growing on the tree of the knowledge of good and evil:

> *And the Lord God commanded the man, saying,*
> *"Of every tree of the garden you may freely eat;*
> *but of the tree of the knowledge of good and evil*
> *you shall not eat, for in the day that you eat of it*
> *you shall surely die"* (Genesis 2:16-17).

God did not create mankind to be a puppet or robot, in spite of what some people think—God and His man fellowshipped on an equal level. God didn't want the kind of relationship where He bossed mankind around like a slave or made him dance to His bidding like a puppet on strings. He wanted mutual closeness.

So He created us with a will of our own. When you think about it, that's pretty risky. God took a chance when He gave us our own free will. But the only *good* relationship is one where each side has a choice to love and cherish the other.

When you love someone, you want them to *want* to love you back, right? Not be forced to walk with you or do your bidding. God loved mankind and wanted mankind to *choose* to love Him back. He tells us in His Word to *choose* life, to choose Him, to choose the blessing. But it's always our choice.

> *I call heaven and earth as witnesses today against you, that I have set before you life and death, blessing and cursing; therefore choose life, that both you and your descendants may live* (Deuteronomy 30:19).
>
> *Choose for yourselves this day whom you will serve…as for me and my house, we will serve the Lord* (Joshua 24:15).

God provided Adam and Eve all the abundance of life in the garden and gave them dominion over the whole earth (see Gen. 1:26). Their part of the covenant was to obey that *one* thing God asked of them—don't eat the fruit from that one tree. That's it. They could eat all the other fruit.

So they had a part to play in this relationship, too. Just like you and I do. Both sides of the relationship had a part—that's what made it balanced and gave each side a choice. You could say that mankind was on probation after Creation—would he keep up his end of the deal?

The Separation

Well, we all know what happened. Mankind did not. We don't know how long they lived in perfect fellowship with God in this wonderful garden He'd created for them, but at some point Eve was deceived by the serpent.

As a result, she and Adam disobeyed and did the one thing God asked them not to do—they ate of the fruit. The moment they did, sin entered the earth. And sin did what it always does—it separated man from God.

> *Now the serpent was more cunning than any beast of the field which the Lord God had made. And he said to the woman, "Has God indeed said, 'You shall not eat of every tree of the garden'?" And the woman said to the serpent, "We may eat the fruit of the trees of the garden; but of the fruit of the tree which is in the midst of the garden, God has said, 'You shall not eat it, nor shall you touch it, lest you die.'" Then the serpent said to the woman, "You will not surely die. For God knows that in the day you eat of it your eyes will be opened, and you will be like God, knowing good and evil." So when the woman saw that*

the tree was good for food, that it was pleasant to the eyes, and a tree desirable to make one wise, she took of its fruit and ate. She also gave to her husband with her, and he ate. Then the eyes of both of them were opened, and they knew that they were naked; and they sewed fig leaves together and made themselves coverings. And they heard the sound of the Lord God walking in the garden in the cool of the day, and Adam and his wife hid themselves from the presence of the Lord God among the trees of the garden. Then the Lord God called to Adam and said to him, "Where are you?" (Genesis 3:1-9)

Think of how tragic this was. Adam and Eve had had perfect, open, loving fellowship with God. When they heard God come walking in the garden every evening, it was their regular practice to run to Him, excited to see Him.

But this time they hid from Him. Suddenly these beings He created for fellowship and communion weren't there. They had been living in perfect communion and light with God, but now they were transformed into beings of the darkness through disobedience. Instantly, because of sin they were in bondage to the enemy.

So he [Adam] said, "I heard Your voice in the garden, and I was afraid because I was naked; and I hid myself." And He said, "Who told you that you were naked? Have you eaten from the tree of which I commanded you that you should not eat?" Then the man said, "The woman whom You gave to be with me, she gave me of the tree, and I ate." And the Lord God said to the woman, "What is this you have done?" The woman said, "The serpent deceived me, and I ate" (Genesis 3:10-13).

I'm not sure that you or I can fully understand the heartbreaking sadness that God experienced as this precious fellowship with His man was broken. This son and daughter He loved so much were now separated from Him. The ones about whom the angels had said:

What is man that You are mindful of him, and the son of man that You visit him? You have made him a little lower than [Yourself] and You have crowned him with glory and honor (Psalm 8:4-5).

God's glorious creation, those He had crowed with glory and honor, who had endless opportunities to know God and commune with Him, were now stolen away by sin, destroying the dream of God. The wages of sin (you could say "the paycheck for sin") is death (see Rom. 6:23), and we have been paying ever since. But it was man himself who allowed death into the earth by disobeying God, and from then on sin has reigned.

Adam and Eve probably didn't even know, at that moment, the ramifications of what they had thrown away. They didn't know that they had doomed all of humankind to be in bondage to sin. But God knew. He knew that sin had stolen away His precious prize, His family. With grief, God drove them out of the garden, effectively separating them from Himself (see Gen. 3:24).

God Makes a Plan

I want you to get just a glimmer of God's heart here. From this moment forward He longed for restored fellowship with His precious creation. This is why He spends the rest of the Old Testament bringing forth a plan to get us back. Why He gives the greatest, most precious thing He has—His only begotten Son—in order to redeem mankind. He loved His creation and wasn't willing to give us up forever.

The heart of the Father never stopped crying out for His sons and daughters. He grieved for 4,000 years. From the moment Adam and Eve sinned, He began looking forward to the day when He could redeem His creation and that lost fellowship and communion could be restored—through the cross.

> *"Come near to Me, hear this: I have not spoken in secret from the beginning; from the time that it was, I was there. And now the Lord God and His Spirit have sent Me." Thus says the Lord, your Redeemer, the Holy One of Israel: "I am the Lord your God, who teaches you to profit, who leads you by the way you should go. Oh, that you had heeded My commandments! Then your peace would have been like a river, and your*

righteousness like the waves of the sea" (Isaiah 48:16-18).

God cried out to His people to follow Him and obey Him, because He wants so much to bless them! Even though He drove Adam out of the garden, He never left him—He was always there. He never stopped taking care of mankind, even when they didn't listen to Him.

I have stretched out My hands all day long to a rebellious people, who walk in a way that is not good, according to their own thoughts (Isaiah 65:2).

He was reaching out His hand to them, but they couldn't respond because of their sinful nature. Light has no fellowship with darkness (see 2 Cor. 6:14). They were completely separated from Him. Their spiritual condition denied them access to fellowship with Almighty God. He still loved them, still wanted to help them and guide them and be their all in all.

But He could not commune with them—He couldn't reach them. For the most part, they didn't understand or even know He was there. It was heartbreaking.

Behind the Veil

During those 4,000 years of separation from mankind, the presence of God on earth lived in a box—the Ark of the Covenant—as I mentioned in the Introduction. He had to separate Himself because we humans, in our sinful condition, could no longer meet face to face with Him.

Throughout the Old Testament many miracles happen surrounding the Ark. The Israelites would often carry it with them into battle to have God's presence on their side, which would guarantee their victory.

When not being carried into battle, the Ark was to be housed in the Tabernacle or the temple, in the center of Jewish life. God still wanted to be in the center of His people's lives, but He had to stay removed from them, dwelling in the Tabernacle, behind a curtain in the Holy of Holies.

The Holy of Holies was the inner room of the Tabernacle (and also the temple). The Mercy Seat sat on top of the Ark (see Exod. 26:34)—it was where God's presence was seated, and from this place He extended mercy to His people when the blood of the atonement was sprinkled once a year on the Day of Atonement (see Lev. 16:15-33). Symbolically, the Mercy Seat protected the Israelites from the judgment of the Law.

This curtain (or veil) separated the Holy of Holies from the rest of the temple (see Heb. 9:1-9) and signified that man was separated from God by sin (see Isa. 59:1-2). Only the High Priest was permitted to pass beyond this veil once each year on the Day of Atonement to enter into God's presence for all of Israel and make atonement for their sins (see Exod. 30:10; Heb. 9:7).

On that day, the High Priest entered into the Holy of Holies and sprinkled the blood of sacrificial animals (a bull offered as atonement for the priest and his household, and a goat offered as atonement for the people) and offered incense upon the Mercy Seat.

By doing this he was paying for his own sins and the sins of all Israel. This act of atonement symbolically brought reconciliation between the people and God, because it's only through the offering of blood that the condemnation of the Law could be taken away and violations of God's laws covered.

On that Day of Atonement, people like you and me had to wait outside the Tabernacle to see if God would accept the sacrifice of blood and our sins would be atoned for the year. That's as close to God as we could get.

So this veil, or curtain, was a type and shadow of the condition of man's fellowship with God. There was separation because of sin. God was inside and man was outside. If any of us had gone into the presence of God, we would have died, because God was completely holy and man was utterly sinful. So for protection, God had to put a barrier between Himself and the ones He loved.

Mankind bore the shame and the bondage of our sin. No matter how hard we tried, we couldn't do right, we couldn't cleanse ourselves from our sin nature through good works or our own efforts. But in Ezekiel 36 our heavenly Father was looking forward to the time when One would come to redeem us:

> *Then I will sprinkle clean water on you, and you shall be clean; I will cleanse you from all your*

filthiness and from all your idols. I will give you
a new heart and put a new spirit within you; I
will take the heart of stone out of your flesh and
give you a heart of flesh. I will put My Spirit
within you and cause you to walk in My statutes,
and you will keep My judgments and do them.
Then you shall dwell in the land that I gave to
your fathers; you shall be My people, and I will
be your God (Ezekiel 36:25-28).

Think about being separated from your loved ones for 4,000 years. That's the picture of God throughout the Old Testament. He longed for the restoration of the fellowship He used to have with His creation. That's why He was working a plan to redeem us. And what a wonderful plan it turned out to be!

Jesus Paid the Price

From the moment that Adam and Eve transgressed the original covenant, all through the Old Testament, we humans could only approach God by shedding the blood of an innocent animal because *"without shedding of blood there is no remission"* of sin (Heb. 9:22). Sin must be judged, and the blood of animals was the payment.

In our sinful state, no human could get close to God. The Old Testament Law was a ministry of wrath, and all our sins were held against us (see Rom. 4:15; 2 Cor. 3:7,9).

This condition of separation between God and His beloved humans could only be rectified by the shedding of perfect blood. The blood of animals would never be enough to completely eradicate sin.

> *The old system under the law of Moses was only a shadow, a dim preview of the good things to come, not the good things themselves. The sacrifices under that system were repeated again and again, year after year, but they were never able to provide perfect cleansing for those who came to worship. If they could have provided perfect cleansing, the sacrifices would have stopped, for the worshipers would have been purified once for all time, and their feelings of guilt would have disappeared* (Hebrews 10:1-2 NLT).

Only the blood of a sinless Lamb could pay the price for our sin. The blood of bulls and goats couldn't do it. Their blood had to continually be shed—it only *covered* sin, it couldn't wash sin away. But the blood of Jesus could do just that. He has *cleansed* us from all unrighteousness (see 1 John 1:9).

This is the scenario into which God sent His only begotten Son—Jesus, the Christ. When Jesus hung on the Cross for you and for me, God placed all of His wrath for the sin of mankind upon Him. This forever satisfied God's wrath. Jesus' blood has washed us clean from sin and made us white as snow (see Isa. 1:18).

By shedding His blood for us on the Cross, Jesus paid the price for our sin in His own body (see 1 Pet. 2:24), and

God quit holding our sin against us. This is exactly what Second Corinthians 5:19 and 21 says:

> *To wit, that God was in Christ, reconciling the world unto himself, not imputing their trespasses unto them; and hath committed unto us the word of reconciliation...For he hath made him to be sin for us, who knew no sin; that we might be made the righteousness of God in him* (KJV).

The word *reconciliation* is talking about making peace. Because of Jesus, God is no longer holding us accountable. Instead, He imputed our sins to Jesus, making Jesus accountable for our sins. *Jesus became what we were so we could become what He was—the righteousness of God.*

I heard one person say it like this: "Jesus was a lightning rod that drew all the judgment of God unto Himself." Think about that! He took it all for us—He was our substitute. He got what we deserved. You and I could never be good enough, never earn and deserve our way back into fellowship with God, but Jesus has done it for us. He actually became sin for us, to make us righteous. Now we are in perfect right standing with God.

God made a way back to Himself 2,000 years ago when Jesus hung on the Cross, and the way is the same today. Jesus said, *"I am the way, the truth, and the life. No one comes to the Father except through Me"* (John 14:6).

The day that Jesus hung on the Cross and bore your sin and mine, the most amazing thing happened! As He hung there, suspended between heaven and earth, beaten, bruised, and dying, separated from God for you and for me, the earth grew dark: *"And Jesus cried out again with a loud voice, and yielded up His spirit. Then, behold, the veil of the temple was torn in two from top to bottom; and the earth quaked..."* (Matt. 27:50-51).

That veil in the Holy Temple, which had stood between God and man for 4,000 years separating the Father from His beloved creation, was torn in two! It was gone! In that instant, from now until then, you and I all of God's family can walk right into His presence to the Holy of Holies.

Jesus' death removed the veil—the sin that had separated all of us from God. That one magnificent act, the summation of God's plan, means we are reunited with our heavenly Father.

> *Come, all you who are thirsty, come to the waters; and you who have no money, come, buy and eat! Come, buy wine and milk without money and without cost. Why spend money on what is not bread, and your labor on what does not satisfy? Listen, listen to me, and eat what is good, and you will delight in the richest of fare. Give ear and come to me; listen, that you may live. I will make an everlasting covenant with you... Seek the Lord while he may be found; call on him while he is near. Let the wicked forsake their ways and the unrighteous their thoughts. Let them turn to the Lord, and he will have mercy on them, and to our God, for he will freely pardon* (Isaiah 55:1-3,6-7 NIV).

Jesus' death, burial, and resurrection marked the end of God's war on sin. The victory has been won! God had made a way to restore fellowship forever through the blood of His precious Son. Peace now reigns between God and man (see Luke 2:13-14).

The Power of the Resurrection

The best news the world has ever received is that Jesus died for our sins. That is the Good News, the Gospel, that you and I are to spread to everyone we know. This is how you and I are able to get close to God.

But think about this: even though He went to the Cross and paid the ultimate price for your sin and mine—and aren't we thankful that He did?—it wouldn't have meant anything if He hadn't risen from the grave.

We are alive because He is alive! Galatians 2:20 says, "*I have been crucified with Christ; it is no longer I who live, but Christ lives in me; and the life which I now live in the flesh I live by faith in the Son of God, who loved me and gave Himself for me.*" This life we now live by faith—as close to God as we want to be—could never have happened if Jesus stayed in the tomb. He would be dead, and we would still be dead in our sin. But He has risen, sprinkled His blood on the Mercy Seat in the Holy of Holies, and that makes all the difference! Our sin was great, but His sacrifice was greater.

Jesus certainly wasn't the first to be crucified. Even though everything about Him was unique—the prophecies of His coming, His birth, His life, the miracles,

His death—it was the resurrection that proved, once and for all, that He was who He said He was. And because He rose from the dead, you and I have also been raised! Because He is alive, we also can live in the light and love of the Father God.

As Christians, the resurrection is the very foundation of what we believe. If there was no resurrection, Christianity is a hoax. But the truth is, it is *the most* significant event in history. It proves, first of all, that Jesus was the Son of God. By rising from the dead, Jesus fulfilled the prophecies and proved His deity. Romans 1:4 declares that *"by being raised from the dead* [Christ] *was proved to be the mighty Son of God, with the holy nature of God himself"* (TLB).

The resurrection is also the proof that our sins are forgiven. The Bible says, *"If Christ has not been raised, your faith is worthless; you are still in your sins"* (1 Cor. 15:17 CSB). The resurrection proved that Jesus had the authority and power to break the bonds of sin, to forgive and bestow eternal life on any person who accepts salvation through Him.

The resurrection means that you and I serve a *living* God. The leader of every other religion in the world is dead. But our Savior is not dead; He is alive! He rose from the dead to sit at God's right hand (see Eph. 1:20). He said in Revelation 1:17-18, *"I am the first and the last, and the Living one; and I was dead, and behold, I am alive for evermore"* (ASV). Your Savior is very much alive and well, and the closer you are to Him, the more of that life you are able to share.

Thankfully, the resurrection also proves that death is not the end. Jesus isn't just a crucifixion survivor. Yes, He died for us, but the crucifixion wasn't the end of the story. He arose! He proved that *death is not the end of human existence.* When our human bodies die on this earth, it's just the beginning of our life in Him! His triumph over death is God's promise that we too shall be raised. Romans 6:9 says, *"Christ rose from the dead and will never die again. Death no longer has any power over him"* (TLB).

The resurrection secured our victory over death as well and *"lifted us up from the grave into glory along with Christ, where we sit with him in the heavenly realms"* (Eph. 2:6 TLB). It proves beyond a shadow of a doubt that Satan is defeated! Colossians 2:15 says, *"And having spoiled principalities and powers, he* [Jesus] *made a shew of them openly, triumphing over them in it"* (KJV). And 1 John 3:8 tells us, *"For this purpose the Son of God was manifested, that He might destroy the works of the devil."*

When Jesus hung on the Cross, Satan thought he had dealt the final blow to God's plan of redemption by killing the Savior. But he was wrong. Because Jesus didn't stay dead! When He rose from the grave, the power of sin and death was forever shattered. Jesus defeated death and hell! Because of the resurrection, you don't ever need to fear Satan again. Through Christ, you and I have victory over sin, death, and the devil in every way.

Think of it this way: Jesus died to something (spiritual death, sickness, and poverty) so you don't have to live with it. He was made poor that you might be rich. By His stripes you are healed. He was made to be sin that you might be made the righteousness of God in Him. Righteousness is not what you have—it is who you have become.

Jesus went somewhere (hell) so you don't have to go. He was and still is your perfect Substitute (see Isa. 53). Your redemption included His death, His burial, and *His resurrection*!

Jesus chose to keep His scars in His resurrected body to remind everyone, including the devil, that He overcame death, hell, and the grave. He is risen! And because He is, so are you. You are seated next to Him at the right hand of God. You are free to get as close to God as you want to.

The Most Important Words in This Book

Now that you've seen how God made a sure way for you to get closer to Him, it's important for me to stop and ask you: have you received Jesus as your Lord and Savior?

Your heavenly Father loves you, has a good plan for your life, and wants to be as close as possible to you—but none of that can happen until you voluntarily join His family by asking Jesus into your heart. That's the way you get "born again"—the way of salvation. There's no other way to be saved from sin (see John 14:6).

Jesus died on the Cross to set you free from sin once and for all—to pay the price you could never pay—but that only happens in *your* life when you invite Him in. You must ask. You must *believe* that He made this sacrifice for you personally, and receive it by saying "yes" to Him, turning over the lordship of your life to Him.

The Bible says that *"whoever calls on the name of the Lord shall be saved"* (Acts 2:21). You must call on Him. Jesus is a gentleman—He's never going to force Himself upon you or make you get saved. As we talked about in Chapter 1, it's always our choice. We have a free will.

And it won't happen automatically, in spite of what some may say. Yes, God is merciful; He loves everyone and wants them to be saved (see 1 Tim. 2:4). But He's waiting for you to ask, to invite Him into your heart. He only comes in when you ask Him. It's the most important thing you'll ever do on this earth.

Look at this list and answer honestly:

1. Have you ever asked Jesus into your heart to be your Lord and Savior?

2. If you died tonight, are you absolutely sure you'd go to heaven?

3. Maybe you asked Him in at one point—are you living today to please Him, letting Him into the very fabric of your life?

If you answered "no" to any of those questions, go to the back of the book and read the page marked "Ask Jesus to Be Your Savior," then pray the prayer you find there. It will change your life forever!

Review in a Nutshell

God made a way through Christ so that the veil of separation has been torn down. Jesus has paid the price for our sin, and all who receive Him as Lord are now righteous in God's sight. Perfect fellowship with God has been restored!

Now Engage:

Read and meditate on the scriptures we've looked at and activate the power of God's Word in your life by speaking these declarations out loud.

> *Then God said, "Let Us make man in Our image, according to Our likeness; let them have dominion over the fish of the sea, over the birds of the air, and over the cattle, over all the earth and over every creeping thing that creeps on the earth"* (Genesis 1:26-27).

Declare:

"From the very beginning of creation, God wanted fellowship with me. It's why He created me in His own image. He originally gave mankind the same power, dominion, and authority in the earth that He had, so we would have that in common with Him. He wanted a family of sons and daughters who would grow up and share His dominion with Him."

Choose for yourselves this day whom you will serve…as for me and my house, we will serve the Lord (Joshua 24:15).

Declare:

"Mankind committed high treason against God and turned dominion of the earth over to Satan. As a result, God became separated from us, hidden behind the veil in the temple. We always have a choice, and I choose to serve, obey, and love God with all my heart."

Thus says the Lord, your Redeemer, the Holy One of Israel: "I am the Lord your God, who teaches you to profit, who leads you by the way you should go. Oh, that you had heeded My commandments! Then your peace would have been like a river, and your righteousness like the waves of the sea" (Isaiah 48:17-18).

Declare:

"God cried out to His people to follow Him and obey Him, because He always wants to bless us. Even though Adam sinned, God never stopped taking care of mankind, even when they didn't listen to Him."

I will cleanse you from all your filthiness and from all your idols. I will give you a new heart and put a new spirit within you; I will take the heart of stone out of your flesh and give you a heart of flesh. I will put My Spirit within you and cause you to walk in My statutes, and you will keep My judgments and do them. Then you shall dwell in the land that I gave to your fathers; you shall be My people, and I will be your God (Ezekiel 36:25-28).

Declare:

"Throughout the whole Old Testament, our heavenly Father was looking forward to the time when Jesus would come to redeem us. He longed for the restoration of the fellowship with His creation. That's why He was working a plan to redeem us. And what a wonderful plan it turned out to be."

The old system under the law of Moses was only a shadow, a dim preview of the good things to come, not the good things themselves. The sacrifices under that system were repeated again and again, year after year, but they were never able to provide perfect cleansing for those who came to worship. If they could have provided perfect cleansing, the sacrifices would have stopped, for the worshipers would have been purified once for all time, and their feelings of guilt would have disappeared (Hebrews 10:1-2 NLT).

Declare:

> "The Old Testament Law was a ministry of wrath and all our sins were held against us. Man could only approach God through the shedding of blood. But only the blood of a sinless Lamb could pay the price for our sin. The blood of bulls and goats couldn't do it. The blood of Jesus could do just that. His blood has cleansed us from all unrighteousness."

God was in Christ, reconciling the world unto himself, not imputing their trespasses unto them; and hath committed unto us the word of reconciliation...For he hath made him to be sin for us, who knew no sin; that we might be made the righteousness of God in him (2 Corinthians 5:19,21 KJV).

Declare:

> "By shedding His blood for me on the Cross, Jesus paid the price for my sin in His own body, and God quit holding my sin against me. He imputed my sin to Jesus, making Jesus accountable for my sin. Jesus became what I was so I could become what He was—the righteousness of God."

And Jesus cried out again with a loud voice, and yielded up His spirit. Then, behold, the veil of the temple was torn in two from top to bottom; and the earth quaked (Matthew 27:50-51).

Declare:

"The moment that Jesus died, the veil in the Holy Temple, which had stood between God and man for 4,000 years separating the Father from His beloved creation, was torn in two! Now all of God's family can walk right into His presence to the Holy of Holies. Jesus' death removed the veil between man and God. There is no more separation."

Give ear and come to me; listen, that you may live. I will make an everlasting covenant with you... Seek the Lord while he may be found; call on him while he is near. Let the wicked forsake their ways and the unrighteous their thoughts. Let them turn to the Lord, and he will have mercy on them, and to our God, for he will freely pardon (Isaiah 55:3,6-7 NIV).

Declare:

"Jesus brought the cry of God's heart to pass, fulfilling what He had been saying all through the Old Testament. Jesus' death, burial, and resurrection marked the end of God's war on sin. The victory has been won! God made a way back for us—restored fellowship forever through the blood of His precious Son. Peace now reigns between God and man."

By being raised from the dead [Christ] *was proved to be the mighty Son of God, with the holy nature of God himself* (Romans 1:4 TLB).

Declare:

"Because Jesus rose from the dead, I have also been raised. Because Jesus is alive, I can also live in the light and love of the Father God. I'm alive because He is alive!"

If Christ has not been raised, your faith is worthless; you are still in your sins (1 Corinthians 15:17 CSB).

Declare:

"The resurrection is proof that my sins are forgiven. It proved that Jesus had the authority and power to break the bonds of sin, to forgive and bestow eternal life on me when I accepted salvation through Him."

Christ rose from the dead and will never die again. Death no longer has any power over him (Romans 6:9 TLB).

Declare:

"The resurrection proves that death is not the end for me. Jesus isn't just a crucifixion survivor.

He arose! He proved that *death is not the end of human existence.* When my body dies on this earth, it's just the beginning of my life in Him. His triumph over death is God's promise that I too shall be raised."

[God] *lifted us up from the grave into glory along with Christ, where we sit with him in the heavenly realms* (Ephesians 2:6 TLB).

Declare:

"The resurrection secured my victory over death. When Jesus rose from the grave, He brought me with Him. I'm seated with God now! I don't ever need to fear Satan again— through Christ, I have victory over him in every way."

Discussion Questions:

How did mankind initially get separated from God? What was the plan He devised to bring us back into fellowship with Him? What does the power of the resurrection mean to you after reading this chapter?

Chapter Three

LOOK AT YOU NOW!

JESUS FOREVER CHANGED THE WAY THAT GOD RELATES TO us. Jesus is the reason that you have a legal right to get closer to God than you ever imagined possible. Look at you—because of Jesus, you're now seated in heavenly places in Christ (see Eph. 2:6)! You're as close to God as the mention of His Name.

You aren't trying to approach God through a veil any more. You have complete access to Him. He has washed you and put His robe of righteousness on you (see Isa. 61:10). Now through Jesus' righteousness you can stand before God and receive His help every day.

You are destined to spend eternity with Him, completely covered with Christ's robe of righteousness. You don't have to wait for the Day of Atonement or bring a blood sacrifice in order to approach Him—you can come to His throne freely, anytime you want. Hebrews 4:14-16 says:

> *Seeing then that we have a great High Priest who*
> *has passed through the heavens, Jesus the Son of*

God, let us hold fast our confession. For we do not have a High Priest who cannot sympathize with our weaknesses, but was in all points tempted as we are, yet without sin. Let us therefore come boldly to the throne of grace, that we may obtain mercy and find grace to help in time of need.

The significance of the veil being removed is so powerful! Jesus became the priest who offered Himself—the perfect and final sacrifice for all. If you believe that and receive Him as your Lord and Savior—the payment for your sin—you never have to be separated from God again! You have total access to Him—you can come boldly before Him.

That means you live by faith in the fact that Jesus has washed your sins away (see Gal. 2:20). He has given you a new nature—you are not an old sinner saved by grace; you are someone completely new (see 2 Cor. 5:17). You have no more shame, no more unworthiness or bondage to sin. That's what allows you to come boldly into God's presence.

This is His doing, not ours (see Ps. 118:22-23). In other words, the only good works we should be doing are Christ's good works. If we mix in our own good works, trying to achieve righteousness by earning it on our own, then we stand before God with stains and holes in our robe, because all of our works are still tainted with sin. We have to realize that access only comes from being righteous in Christ's righteousness. We must believe completely in the price that Jesus paid.

You Are Worthy

Sometimes we still have feelings of inadequacy and we try to hide from God. When we goof up, we're tempted to give in to shame and *not* approach Him boldly. We still *feel* unclean and undeserving. After all, we know the thoughts that run through our heads. We know the inappropriate conversations we've had. We know the things we've done that fall short of pleasing God. It's easy to feel inadequate in the presence of our holy God.

But because of what Jesus did for us, we're not inadequate! We are worthy! Not one of us is worthy on our own, by our own works (see Ps. 14:1). Romans 3:10 says, *"There is none righteous, no, not one."* But when God sent Jesus *"to seek and to save that which was lost"* (Luke 19:10), everything changed! Instead of judgment, we received grace! Instead of destruction, we received salvation! Instead of death, we received life!

First John 2:2 says, *"And he is the propitiation* [that is, total satisfaction] *for our sins: and not for ours only, but also for the sins of the whole world"* (KJV). God made us worthy when He put His Son upon the Cross at Calvary—when He put our sin (and the penalties for sin) upon Jesus Himself. God made us worthy when He took the righteousness of Jesus Himself and put it upon us (see 2 Cor. 5:21). It was the Great Substitution. Now God sees us not in our sin, but in the righteousness of Christ.

No matter what you've done (or haven't done), the blood of Jesus was enough to make you righteous. *You* don't have to pay for sin—it's already paid for. Today if you sin, 1 John 1:9 tells you what to do: *"If we confess our sins, He is faithful and just to forgive us our sins and to cleanse us from all unrighteousness."* Your part is to genuinely repent, ask God's forgiveness, then believe you receive it. It's what Jesus died for.

The devil would love you to think your actions have disqualified you. But he's a liar. God's plans for you haven't changed (see Jer. 29:11; Rom. 11:29). His power in you is greater than anything you've done (or not done). He loves you more than the devil hates you! He forgives you, and His mercy endures *forever.*

The righteousness of Christ is freely given to us when we *believe*—when we completely trust what God has said and what Jesus has done. Believe that you're wearing Jesus' robe of righteousness. You've been made righteous in His sight! When you know this and remember how He sees you, the magnitude of His love makes you want to approach Him and to please Him. When you goof up, run *to* the throne, not away from it! He's awaiting you with open arms.

See, God loves you in spite of your shortcomings and your inadequacies. He's cleansed you from *all* unrighteousness. You have complete access to Him. He wants to help you, love you, and allow you to partake of His grace every day. There is an unending supply of His supernatural wisdom, resources, and ability available for you.

You don't need an appointment to meet with Him. You have a standing appointment! He's never disinterested in your life or your concerns. He doesn't want you to feel uncomfortable around Him. He's not too busy to meet with you—He can love, cherish, nurture and help countless billions of people all at the same time! He's not a human who has limitations—He's God. He's omnipresent—He's everywhere at once. When you understand by faith just how close you can get to Him, you'll find His fellowship, comfort, peace, direction, and love waiting for you at every turn.

Just look at you now! You were originally created in the image of God but were separated from Him by sin. Now that Jesus has gone to the Cross and you have received Him as your Lord and Savior, you have been restored to perfect fellowship! You're a brand-new creation in Christ, made in the image of God. Second Corinthians 5:17 says, *"If anyone is in Christ, he is a new creation; old things have passed away; behold, all things have become new."*

The first Adam committed high treason against God and plunged all of us into sin. But the second Adam redeemed us. First Corinthians says, *"Just as everyone dies because we all belong to Adam, everyone who belongs to Christ will be given new life"* (1 Cor. 15:22 NLT). *"The first man Adam became a living being; the last Adam became a life-giving spirit"* (1 Cor. 15:45 CSB).

Jesus is called the Second Adam because in Him everything that the first Adam had with God was restored to us. Everything! That means that now you're in perfect position to fellowship with God. You can get as close to Him as you want, because you stand before Him righteous.

You and I could never be good enough to become righteous on our own, but Jesus kept all the commandments for us. Then He offered His righteousness to us. Our part is now to simply trust in what He has done for us—to clothe ourselves in His beautiful robe of righteousness. It is the most important thing you can ever do.

You Are God's Son or Daughter

Because Jesus' finished work on the Cross has given us direct access to God, we can now enter into His presence as children, not as servants or slaves. Second Corinthians 6:18 says, *"I will be a Father to you, and you shall be My sons and daughters, says the Lord Almighty."* Think about it. Children have privileges in a household. They don't stand outside the house and knock—they come right in, because their dad owns the house.

They don't stand outside the kitchen and ask for food—they go right into the refrigerator and help themselves. If you or I were a guest in someone's house, it would be considered rude if we just walked in without knocking—without waiting to be invited. If we just walked up to their fridge and started eating things out of it, we would be outside our rights as our guest—and we'd probably get some dirty looks too!

I remember when I moved back into my hometown after I was married, and I needed a particular tool or something, I'd just go over to my parents' house during the day (when they were at work) and borrow the tool. Why?

Because I was their child and I was perfectly confident in believing that everything that was theirs was mine. Now, if I weren't their child—if I was just a friend or a guest—that could be called stealing! But children have certain rights and privileges in a family.

Guests don't have the same kind of access as children do. You are no longer a guest in God's house—you are His beloved child. First John 3:1 says, *"See how very much our Father loves us, for he calls us his children, and that is what we are!"* (NLT). He loves you! That love gives you the kind of access that only family can have. You don't have to wait to be invited—you can legally now just walk in boldly and claim your rights and privileges. You can expect to be welcomed with open arms. You can crawl up into Daddy's lap and cuddle up for a nice chat.

When I found out I was truly God's beloved daughter, I realized I didn't have to start out conversations with Him like, "Almighty One, please hear me," or "Sir, can I speak with You for a moment?" No, I can just say, "Abba, Father..." and continue talking with Him as the apple of His eye—as if He *wanted* to hear from me and have a chat with me.

Because He does! And He wants to do the same with you. As His beloved child, bought by the blood of the Lamb, you no longer have to shake with fear when talking to God, wondering if you'll be received or not, as people did in the Old Testament. You have right standing—you are the righteousness of God in Christ (see Rom. 6:18)!

You are God's beloved child, with all the rights and privileges that entails.

Your Identity in Christ

Sometimes we've had really rotten things happen in our life that have shaped our self-image. Yes, there are some of us who had a great childhood and have always had a fairly healthy self-image. But maybe you're one whose family or childhood friends (or enemies!) said and did things that made you doubt your worth. Maybe you have a bad self-image. That can make it much harder to get close to God.

Many times when we have a bad self-image, we take it out on others. We can be controlling, judgmental, critical, manipulative, angry, negative, and overbearing. We're miserable in our own skin, and we're making everyone around us miserable too. When you see someone who is acting like that, it often means that they have a bad self-image. As the saying goes, "Hurt people hurt people."

But life doesn't have to be that way. When you become a Christian, the life of God comes to live inside you (see Rom. 8:10). Ephesians 2:10 says, *"For we are God's masterpiece. He has created us anew in Christ Jesus"* (NLT), so you can do the good things He's planned for you. You're simply not the same person on the inside that you were before.

In reality, becoming a Christian means receiving a new identity in Christ. You don't *lose* your true self in Jesus; you *become* your true self in Him. He is your life (see Col. 3:4). Acts 17:28 says, *"In Him we live and move and have our being."* When you are born again after receiving Jesus as Savior, He puts His very Spirit in your spirit as His guarantee of everything you have inherited in Him.

The Holy Spirit is your surety—your proof—of everything that you now have and everything that you now are:

> *In Him you also trusted, after you heard the word of truth, the gospel of your salvation; in whom also, having believed, you were sealed with the Holy Spirit of promise, who is the guarantee of our inheritance until the redemption of the purchased possession, to the praise of His glory* (Ephesians 1:13-14).

> *Now He who establishes us with you in Christ and has anointed us is God, who also has sealed us and given us the Spirit in our hearts as a guarantee* (2 Corinthians 1:21-22).

> *Now He who has prepared us for this very thing is God, who also has given us the Spirit as a guarantee* (2 Corinthians 5:5).

When God gave us the Holy Spirit, it was His "down payment" on all His promises—the promise of heaven, surely, but also of all the benefits *now,* on earth, of everything He is and everything He has. That means His joy becomes our joy; His love becomes our love; His peace is our peace; His strength is our strength; His health is our health; His provision is our provision. And more!

There is nothing more amazing than being in Christ, being His child, the heir of His inheritance (see Rom. 8:17).

No more do you ever need to walk under a blanket of shame or unworthiness with a bad self-image. Romans 8:1 says, *"There is therefore now no condemnation to those who are in Christ Jesus."* In Christ, you are new.

You simply must believe it. You must *believe* that you are who God says you are, not what others say or what has happened to you in the past. See yourself as God sees you today. The best way to do that is to look into His Word, the Bible. His Word will tell you who you really are!

The Bible is described as a mirror (see James 1:23). Instead of looking into your mirror and seeing who you have been, look instead into God's mirror and see yourself as He does! He sees you *in Christ.* When you look at yourself through God's eyes, you see a wonderful new creation, bought by the blood of Jesus, beloved in your Father's sight.

I know that's easier said than done. There are plenty of born-again believers who are saved and love God, but they don't know who they are in Christ. They might know they'll go to heaven when they die, but they have no peace or joy or victory or provision in their everyday life. They still feel guilty, unworthy, lacking, insecure, or condemned all the time.

When people feel like that, they often try to gain a sense of self-worth by working for it—by earning or deserving it. They attempt to find their identity in what they *do* or in things and people instead of looking to Jesus alone. That kind of life leads to frustration, misery, and burnout, because

Jesus has paid the price for our total deliverance, but we haven't fully received His gracious gift.

Receive It by Faith

There is a way to receive God's gift and change how you see yourself. Second Corinthians 5:7 says, *"For we walk by faith, not by sight [living our lives in a manner consistent with our confident belief in God's promises]"* (AMP). We do it by faith—by believing what God has said.

Read that verse again, and this time, ask yourself what you truly believe about your *relationship with God.* Do you truly believe He loves you? Many of us think He loves us, but only if we're doing all the right things. That's a trap, because Jesus has already done all the work to make you righteous! Because of the blood of Jesus, God's love for you is *unconditional.* That means He loves you *no matter what* you do or don't do.

Now, don't misunderstand me—it does matter what you do and how you act. Your works and your actions don't earn you salvation, but as a Christian you are to look and act different from the world, because you have the Greater One in you (see 1 John 4:4)!

The book of Ephesians is helpful in explaining this. The first three chapters are about what you have in Christ—who you are in Him and all that has been given to you as His beloved child. Then the last three chapters are about what do now—how to "walk worthy of your calling in Christ" (see Eph. 4:1).

But none of that changes your right standing with God or His love for you. You are righteous in Jesus' righteousness, and God loves you because He is good, not because you are! You are washed clean by the blood (see Isa. 1:18), and He loves you if you never do another thing right. He loves you with no strings attached—not based on your performance, but based on what the blood of Jesus has bought for you. That will never change.

When you truly see that and receive that revelation by faith, you can be emotionally healed and restored. You can begin to develop a new, healthy image of yourself with your identity in Christ, because you are perfectly loved!

The way to get there is to soak your mind and your spirit with the truth of God's Word. *"Faith comes by hearing, and hearing by the word of God"* (Rom. 10:17). Faith for anything—including believing who you are in Christ—comes from God's Word. Reading and meditating on what God says about you is the only way to change the way you think about yourself and develop a self-image in line with who you really are in Christ. (We'll talk more about daily time with Him in Chapter 6.)

Romans 12:2 says, *"Do not be conformed to this world, but be transformed by the renewing of your mind, that you may prove what is that good and acceptable and perfect will of God."* You've already been transformed on the inside by the blood of Jesus, being made a new creature. But the way that becomes a reality to you is by the way you think. You must think of yourself as righteous. You do that by renewing your mind to what God says about you in His Word.

The word *renew* means to "regenerate" or to "rebuild." Before you were a Christian, you thought of yourself one way. If you had a bad self-image, you thought of yourself badly—undeserving, inadequate, unworthy. Now that you're born again, it's time to regenerate those thoughts! To rebuild them into the same thoughts that God has toward you.

If you've had a bad self-image or struggled to believe that God really sees you as righteous and loves you unconditionally, use the declarations at the end of this chapter to read and speak out the scriptures we've talked about in this chapter. They are truth! As you read and meditate on them, it will get down into your spirit and you'll begin to see yourself the way God sees you. You will begin to live in your new identity in Christ.

He'll Never Leave You

We've seen that God never wanted to withhold His presence from mankind, and now we know that He certainly will never again withhold it from those of us who are redeemed by the blood of Jesus! You may have heard people say that sometimes God is silent—that there are times when He withdraws Himself from us.

But that's not true! When you can't "feel" God's presence with you or in you, religious teaching says that He's just disappeared or maybe wandered away from you, disinterested in your problems. That's the same mentality that says that if you do a bunch of good works and try to earn back His favor, He'll show up again. What sad, incorrect thinking that is.

When Jesus died on the Cross, He became your substitute in every way. In other words, whatever He bore, you don't ever have to bear again! Jesus bore our sickness so we no longer have to bear it (see 1 Pet. 2:24). He bore our poverty that we might be rich and we no longer have to bear poverty (see 2 Cor. 8:9).

In that same way, we no longer have to bear the separation that came from sin. In Matthew 27:46, the Bible says that Jesus bore separation from God. In those last minutes of His life, He cried out, *"My God, My God, why have You forsaken Me?"* He had never been separated from the presence of His Father—what a desperate feeling that must have been for Him.

But He did it for you and for me. God had not removed His presence here. When sin came on Jesus (for us) He could no longer perceive His Father's presence because *sin is what separates.* Jesus took on Himself our sin that caused separation, and once He did that meant we no longer have to be separated. Think about that!

Jesus made the way for you to be as close as you want to God. What an unspeakable gift!

When Jesus died on the Cross, God was on the edge of His seat, because He was about to get to do what He had waited 4,000 years to do—bring us back into perfect fellowship with Him. Jesus cried out with a loud voice, *"It is finished!"* (John 19:30), and that meant the separation was finished! The price for sin had been paid, communion with God was completely restored. That veil was torn down— no more keeping man out of the presence of God.

God had hated that veil. He'd hated that separation from His creation, denied the fellowship and communion He craved to have with us. He'd hated that veil for 4,000 years. And now it was gone, once and for all! Now the way to His throne was completely cleared.

Don't ever let anyone tell you that God is far from you or that He doesn't want you. Don't let anyone convince you that He has left you or is displeased with you. He worked for 4,000 years to bring you back into perfect fellowship with Him. He gave His most precious gift to buy you—His only begotten Son (see 1 Pet. 1:18-19).

Just look at you now! He will never ever withhold His presence from you. The devil may try to keep you from Him, your flesh may fight you, but God is on your side. Hebrews 10:21-23 says:

> *And having a High Priest over the house of God, let us draw near with a true heart in full assurance of faith, having our hearts sprinkled from an evil conscience and our bodies washed with pure water. Let us hold fast the confession of our hope without wavering, for He who promised is faithful.*

You can draw near with assurance. He is faithful! Ever since the veil was torn, God has been saying "draw near"— He's been calling out to us for fellowship. The way is open!

It's our choice. I encourage you to draw near. The door to His throne is open, and you are welcome there. Not crawling on your knees, but walking in with head held high. Jesus paid your entrance, once for all.

He's waiting for you. He's not there impatiently tapping His foot, waiting for you to get it all together or get cleaned up before you come to Him. He wants you as you are—right now. He knew you and wanted you long before you ever knew or wanted Him. He sees you as righteous. He loves you. He wants to help you. He's made sure there's a way for you to come in, to get as close as you want to Him. You belong in His presence in a way that no other being has ever belonged.

Review in a Nutshell

Because of what Jesus did for you on the Cross, you are worthy—you're God's son or daughter, completely righteous in His sight, with complete access to Him, and your identity is in Christ.

Now Engage:

Read and meditate the scriptures we've looked at, and activate the power of God's Word in your life by speaking these declarations out loud.

> *I will greatly rejoice in the Lord, my soul shall be joyful in my God; for He has clothed me with the garments of salvation, He has covered me with the robe of righteousness* (Isaiah 61:10).

Declare:

> "Jesus is the reason I have a legal right to get closer to God. Because of Him, I'm seated in heavenly places in Christ! I have complete access. Jesus has washed away my sin and put His robe of righteousness on me. Through Jesus' righteousness I can stand before God and receive His help every day."

> *And he* [Jesus] *is the propitiation* [that is, total satisfaction] *for our sins: and not for ours only, but also for the sins of the whole world* (1 John 2:2 KJV).

Declare:

"God made me worthy when He put my sin upon Jesus on the Cross. He took the righteousness of Jesus Himself and put it upon me. It was the Great Substitution. Now God sees me not in my sin, but in the righteousness of Christ. No matter what I've done (or haven't done), the blood of Jesus was enough to make me righteous. I don't have to pay the penalty for sin—it's already paid for."

If we confess our sins, He is faithful and just to forgive us our sins and to cleanse us from all unrighteousness (1 John 1:9).

Declare:

"Today if I sin, I will genuinely repent, ask God's forgiveness, then believe I receive it. This is what Jesus died for. The devil wants me to think I'm disqualified, but he's a liar. God's plans for me haven't changed. His power in me is greater than anything I've done (or not done). He loves me more than the devil hates me! He forgives me, and His mercy endures forever."

If anyone is in Christ, he is a new creation; old things have passed away; behold, all things have become new (2 Corinthians 5:17).

Declare:

> "Now that Jesus has gone to the Cross and I've received Him as my Lord and Savior, I've been restored to perfect fellowship with God. I'm a brand-new creation in Christ, made in the image of God. He loves me in spite of my shortcomings and inadequacies—He's cleansed me from *all* unrighteousness."

> *Just as everyone dies because we all belong to Adam, everyone who belongs to Christ will be given new life* (1 Corinthians 15:22 NLT).
>
> *The first man Adam became a living being; the last Adam became a life-giving spirit* (1 Corinthians 15:45 CSB).

Declare:

> "The first Adam committed high treason against God and plunged all of us into sin. But the second Adam redeemed us. Jesus is called the Second Adam, because in Him everything that the first Adam had with God was restored to us. Everything! That means that now I'm in perfect position to fellowship with God. I can get as close to Him as I want, because I stand before Him righteous."

> *I will be a Father to you, and you shall be My sons and daughters, says the Lord Almighty* (2 Corinthians 6:18).

Declare:

> "I'm not a guest or a stranger in God's house—
> I'm His beloved child with all the rights and
> privileges that entails. I have privileges in the
> household, because my heavenly Dad owns the
> house! I don't have to wonder if I'll be received
> or not—I'm God's child, I have right standing,
> I am the righteousness of God in Christ."

> *See how very much our Father loves us, for he
> calls us his children, and that is what we are!* (1
> John 3:1 NLT)

Declare:

> "My Father loves me! That love gives me the
> kind of access that only family can have. I don't
> have to wait to be invited into God's pres-
> ence—I can legally walk in boldly and claim
> my rights and privileges. I can expect to be
> welcomed with open arms. He *wants* to talk
> with me and answer my prayers. I'm the apple
> of His eye!"

> *For we are God's masterpiece. He has created
> us anew in Christ Jesus, so we can do the good
> things he planned for us long ago* (Ephesians
> 2:10 NLT).

Declare:

> "When I became a Christian, the life of God came to live inside me. I'm not the same person on the inside that I was before—I have a new identity in Christ. I am His masterpiece, doing the good things He has planned for me. I haven't lost my true self; I've become my true self."

Now He who has prepared us for this very thing is God, who also has given us the Spirit as a guarantee (2 Corinthians 5:5).

Declare:

> "When I received Jesus as Savior, He put His very Spirit in my spirit as His guarantee of everything I've inherited in Him. The Holy Spirit is the 'down payment' on all God's promises to me—His joy is my joy; His love is my love; His peace is my peace; His strength is my strength; His health is my health; His provision is my provision, and more!"

There is therefore now no condemnation to those who are in Christ Jesus (Romans 8:1).

Declare:

> "Never again do I need to walk under a blanket of shame or unworthiness with a bad self-image. I am new in Christ! I am His child, the heir of His inheritance. I believe it. I am who

God says I am, not what others say or what has happened in my past. I see myself as God sees me."

Do not be conformed to this world, but be transformed by the renewing of your mind, that you may prove what is that good and acceptable and perfect will of God (Romans 12:2).

Declare:

"I've already been transformed on the inside by the blood of Jesus, being made a new creature. Now I will change the way I think about myself by reading and meditating on what God says about me. This will help me to renew my mind and develop a self-image in line with who I really am in Christ."

Discussion Questions:

Have you ever felt unworthy or had a bad image since becoming a Christian? Do you feel differently now that you've read this chapter? What does God's Word say about your worthiness? How can you change the image you have of yourself?

Chapter Four

AMAZING LOVE

ONE THING THAT KEEPS US FROM GETTING CLOSER TO GOD IS not understanding or believing how much He loves us. The book of First John is an excellent place to read more about the love of God. If you're having trouble believing God loves you, spend a lot of time reading and meditating in First John.

The truth is, God absolutely adores you. You have never been loved like this before! But you have to believe it. First John 4:16 says, *"And we have known and believed the love that God has for us. God is love, and he who abides in love abides in God, and God in him."* You can't abide with Him, get close to Him, without believing the love He has for you.

That "Love Thing"

Sometimes it's hard for us to imagine how much God loves us. In reality, most of us know ourselves too well to believe it! Too many Christians believe in God all right, but they don't know that the entire intent of His heart toward us is good—everything He does is born out of His love.

I came to that realization one day when I was teaching a class at the Bible school where I was an instructor for nine years. I was substituting for another teacher and decided to just teach on God's love, because it's one of my favorite subjects and because most people need to hear it more! That day, all 300 students in the class were open and receptive, and I believe God really moved on their hearts.

Afterward a woman came up to me, and I wasn't sure why, but she began to give me her educational resume. She told me she had a degree from this university in theology and a master's degree from that university in world religions, plus a graduate's seminary degree from such and such a place. I have to admit, I got a little bit intimidated, and was glad I hadn't known all that *before* I taught!

But I also wondered why in the world she was reading me the laundry list of her accomplishments—what did all her degrees have to do with God's love? It became clearer as she finally said, "So I have all these degrees and religious education, but this 'love thing' you talked about—I don't have that. I don't really understand how God can love *me*."

I managed to keep my mouth from dropping open. Can you imagine, all those hours of study and all that hard work, yet she'd missed the "love thing"—she'd missed the *main thing!* All that education, and she'd missed the whole reason that God had created us and then bought us back with the precious blood of His only Son. She'd missed the whole point of John 3:16: *"For God so loved the world that He gave His only begotten Son, that whoever believes in Him should not perish but have everlasting life."*

The Bible says that God doesn't just *have* love—He *is* love! *"Beloved, let us love one another, for love is of God; and everyone who loves is born of God and knows God. He who does not love does not know God, for God is love"* (1 John 4:7-8). He is the very essence of love—His whole being is love. That means His entire motivation toward mankind is love. He is the lover of our souls. Without Him, there is no love at all.

My heart went out to this woman and all her various degrees. I could tell that just from that short 50-minute teaching about God's great love, her heart was crying out for it. She wanted to know more—she wanted to know Him!

I took some time with her, explaining as best I could in a short time just how much God loved her and wanted to be close to her. I prayed with her to receive Jesus and gave her my sermon notes so she'd have the references to a lot of love scriptures—I encouraged her to meditate on them and get them deep into her heart. She left that classroom looking much brighter than when she had first approached me. She was beginning to see that God knew her personally and loved her endlessly, and it made all the difference!

A God-Shaped Void

We humans were created to love—it's how God made us. Specifically, we were created to love *Him* and to fellowship with Him. Every person has a God-shaped void on the inside of them, a place that only He can fill. Psalm 42:1 says, *"As the deer pants for the water brooks, so pants my soul for You, O God."* Our souls crave fellowship and closeness with our Creator.

A lot of people don't know what their souls are thirsting for, so they try to fill the void with something else—entertainment, alcohol, drugs, or other people, for example. But nothing else will fulfill that gaping void in their hearts but a relationship with the One who created them. Every person's heart continually cries out to know their Creator.

Here's the thing that we humans have so much trouble understanding—God loves us because He is love, not because we're so loveable. He loves us because *He* is good, not because we are. We cannot earn and deserve this love. We can only receive it and believe it. And we know that is possible because 1 John 4:16 says, *"And we have known and believed the love that God has for us."*

Your Father God knows everything about you—the good, the bad, and the ugly—and He loves you anyway. In Jeremiah 31:3 He says, *"I have loved you with an everlasting love; therefore with lovingkindness I have drawn you."* Now, when God says "everlasting" He really means it. Nothing in this world lasts forever—except His love for you. It will never change, never go away based on your performance. You are loved with an everlasting love. Period.

I know it sounds too good to be true, but it *is* true, so you might as well come to grips with it! Purpose today to believe it and receive it.

Too Much Grace?

There are many, many Christians who can't embrace this all-encompassing love of God. They believe that you can't tell someone "God still loves you" if that person continually lives in sin. Many preachers angrily talk about "greasy grace"—meaning doing whatever your flesh wants, acting however you want, living in perpetual sin, selling out to the world, yet "sliding into heaven" on God's grace.

They argue that extending too much grace (too much "God still loves you anyway") gives people an excuse for acting like the devil and not walking in the holiness that God has called us to as believers.

But there's no such thing as "too much grace." Grace is real. You were saved by grace! Ephesians 2:8-9 says, *"For by grace you have been saved through faith, and that not of yourselves; it is the gift of God, not of works, lest anyone should boast."*

Christians who use grace as an excuse to sin have missed the entire point of grace. The Bible tells us exactly what this grace is for: *"For the grace of God that brings salvation has appeared to all men, teaching us that, denying ungodliness and worldly lusts, we should live soberly, righteously, and godly in the present age"* (Titus 2:11-12). Grace is not an excuse to sin—grace helps us to deny ungodliness and lust so we can live soberly and righteously and godly, right now in the 21st century!

Christians are empowered from within by God's grace to withstand temptation and walk in a way that honors and pleases Him. We can't do it on our own, but we don't have to! He's given us His grace to help us do it.

So the question remains: does God still love us if we sin? The answer is *yes!* His love is not based on what you or I *do* or how we act—it's based on His covenant with us through the blood of Jesus. That blood was the payment for sin, and it has never lost its power.

"Are you saying, Karen, that if someone commits a heinous crime or lies or cheats or steals tomorrow, God would still love them?" Yes. Don't get me wrong—sin still separates, and what you sow, you will reap (see Gal. 6:7), so sin is always a bad idea. There will be ramifications of sin. For example, if someone robs a jewelry store and they get caught, they'll go to prison. Even if they did rob a jewelry store, or lied, cheated, or stole, God would absolutely still love them.

But here's the question we have to ask: does that person love God?

God loves us no matter what, but what is the intent of the heart? If someone is purposefully committing sins right and left or willfully disobeying God's instructions, I would have to say they don't love God. They might say they're Christians, but they haven't given their life to Jesus as He gave His to them. They're still living for the lust of their flesh and for their own selfish desires. Their heart is not His.

God is all about *our hearts*. As the old saying goes, salvation is free, but it costs you your life. God wants all of you. He wants your heart.

It's All About the Heart

Remember how, way back in the Old Testament, God wanted to be closer to us? He wanted us to adhere to more than laws written on tablets—He wanted to be in our hearts so He could love us and we would love Him. He looked forward to the day when our hearts would be one with His again:

> *Behold, the days are coming, says the Lord, when I will make a new covenant with the house of Israel and with the house of Judah—not according to the covenant that I made with their fathers in the day that I took them by the hand to lead them out of the land of Egypt, My covenant which they broke, though I was a husband to them, says the Lord. But this is the covenant that I will make with the house of Israel after those days, says the Lord: I will put My law in their minds, and write it on their hearts; and I will be their God, and they shall be My people* (Jeremiah 31:31-33).

The Bible calls King David, Israel's greatest king, "a man after God's own heart" (see 1 Sam. 13:14). It's why, even after David sinned by sleeping with another man's wife and then having that man killed, God forgave him when he repented and still called him a man after His own heart in the New Testament (see Acts 13:22). God loved David's heart toward Him.

But the same wasn't true with David's son Solomon. First Kings 11:4 says, *"For it was so, when Solomon was old, that his wives turned his heart after other gods; and his heart was not loyal to the Lord his God, as was the heart of his father David."* To God, that was the worst thing that could happen—He lost Solomon's heart.

You can see from theses verses that God's heart is toward mankind. He did everything in His power to bring us back to His heart—He sent Jesus. All He wants from us in return is to believe what He's done through Jesus and to love Him with all *our* hearts!

Loving and serving God is what we do in response to His love. Someone who purposefully and perpetually sins is someone who is not responding to God's great love— someone who is not believing everything Jesus has done for them and whose heart is not after God's heart. Christians who try to see how much they can get away with and still make heaven—who say, "It doesn't mattes what I do, I'm saved by grace"—are Christians who don't love God.

Those who love God live to please Him! Those who love God are seeking His heart, listening to His voice, and endeavoring to stay close to Him. Those who love God understand the price that Jesus paid to set them *free* from the bondage of sin—why would anyone go back to it? And again, sin still does what it's always done—it separates. I don't ever *want* to be separated from God!

The closer I get to Him, the more I love Him because I find out more and more about His love for me. That makes me want to live and walk worthy of Him. He has given His all for me. I want my life to please and bless His Daddy-heart. How about you?

Supernatural Love

One of my favorite "love" scriptures is First Corinthians 13:4-8 in the Amplified Bible, Classic Edition. Just as the name suggests, this version of the Bible *amplifies* the scripture—it elaborates and expands these truths to give us even more insight into God's heart.

There is so much to be found in this section of scripture that I used to make my Bible school classes memorize it, and then we would say it aloud together every morning before class. Because I truly believe that understanding God's love for us and then walking in that love with others is a huge key to success in life and ministry. To this day, I still have former students tell me how years later this scripture will rise up in their hearts and help them in any number of situations in their life.

So let's read it. Now, the first time through, read it with the thought in your head, "This is the God-kind of love. It's supernatural. This is how God loves me." Ready? Read:

> *Love endures long and is patient and kind; love never is envious nor boils over with jealousy, is not boastful or vainglorious, does not display itself haughtily.*
>
> *It is not conceited* (arrogant and inflated with pride); *it is not rude* (unmannerly) *and does not*

act unbecomingly. Love (God's love in us) does not insist on its own rights or its own way, for it is not self-seeking; it is not touchy or fretful or resentful; it takes no account of the evil done to it [it pays no attention to a suffered wrong].

It does not rejoice at injustice and unrighteousness, but rejoices when right and truth prevail.

Love bears up under anything and everything that comes, is ever ready to believe the best of every person, its hopes are fadeless under all circumstances, and it endures everything [without weakening].

Love never fails [never fades out or becomes obsolete or comes to an end].

In a nutshell, God's love for you is enduring—He is patient with you (not irritated) and He is kind to you. (Ephesians 2:7 says that He will spend all eternity showing us *"the exceeding riches of His grace in His kindness toward us in Christ Jesus."*) He's never envious or boastful or haughty in His attitude toward you.

God is not prideful or rude and He's not out for His own good—He's out for yours. He's not touchy and He's not keeping track of your mistakes. He doesn't rejoice when things go badly for you—He rejoices when right and truth prevail in your life!

His love for you bears up under anything and everything that comes in your relationship—He always believes the best of you. He has high hopes for you in every circumstance and

His love for you carries through every time without weakening. He will never stop loving you—ever.

If you've ever struggled with the notion that God loves you and wants to be close to you, I encourage you to use the declarations at the end of this chapter often. It will help you to meditate on these truths and speak them out to take hold of them for your own life so it gets down in your heart once and for all that you are truly loved.

Your Turn

Now let's read this wonderful section of scripture one more time, except this time, read it with the thought, "This is how I can walk in love with others. This is the God-kind of love that's flowing in *me*." I know that might seem impossible, but remember this is a supernatural love we're talking about—you're not mustering up this love on your own. Romans 5:5 says *"the love of God has been poured out in* [your heart] *by the Holy Spirit."*

I want you to know that the Holy Spirit did a good job when He poured God's love into your heart. I've had people say to me, "Well, I just don't feel that much love, Karen— I'm not a real loving person." But this kind of love is not a feeling—it's a *choice*. If you're a Christian, the Bible says God's love is in you—you have it all! The Holy Spirit didn't give you just a partial load. It's just up to you to choose to believe it and yield to it.

I once handed this verse to a young woman who had come to my office for counseling about a couple of relationships. I wanted her to see that her relationships could be different if she embraced the truths in these verses.

She quickly scanned the page and then quickly put the paper back down on the desk saying, "Well, that would be nice, but it doesn't have anything to do with what I'm telling you." She didn't accept one word as truth—she rejected the entire idea that love was the answer to her problems.

Don't let that be you! Instead, let's read this again together, believing that this love is flowing to us and *through us*. This time, let's personalize it by making it the completion of this sentence: "Because God's love is in me...

> *I endure long and I'm patient and kind; I'm never is envious or boil over with jealousy, I'm not boastful or vainglorious, I don't display myself haughtily.*
>
> *I'm not conceited (arrogant or inflated with pride); I'm not rude or unmannerly and I don't act unbecomingly. I don't insist on my own rights or my own way, for I'm not self-seeking. I'm not touchy or fretful or resentful; I take no account of the evil done to me [I pay no attention to a suffered wrong].*
>
> *I do not rejoice at injustice and unrighteousness, but rejoice when right and truth prevail.*
>
> *I bear up under anything and everything that comes, am ever ready to believe the best of every person, my hopes are fadeless under all*

circumstances, and I endures everything [without weakening].

I never fail [never fade out or become obsolete or come to an end].

Just imagine living your life like this! You'd never be hurt or offended because you're not keeping track—you're not selfish or fretful; you're always believing the best of everyone. You could bear up under anything and everything that comes! Living a life full of God's love is a life of peace and freedom.

Try This Test

God's love for you is so much greater than you can even imagine. It's deeper than anything you've ever experienced. I'll prove it—try this test. Take a moment and think of a person you love with all your heart. Say to them, "My love for you is patient. I'm never impatient with you—I never have been. I've never shown you impatience of any kind."

Then say to them, "I love you so much that I'm always kind to you. I haven't ever spoken an unkind word to you. I've never had an unkind thought toward you." This is a hard test, isn't it? Try saying all those things from First Corinthians 13 to the one you love: "I've never been envious of you; never felt jealous of anything you have or your abilities. I've never been resentful or spoken rudely to you."

Keep going: "I never insist on my own rights or my own ways; I've never been angry with you; I've never kept track of anything you've done that hurt me—I've not paid any attention, and I've wiped them out of my memory for all time. My love for you never gives up, never loses faith, never stops believing the best in you. I haven't given in to despair or discouragement. My love for you endures through every circumstance—it never fails."

How did you do? This is love's standard—*this is how God loves us.* Read those last three paragraphs again and imagine God thinking of *you,* saying those words to you.

You've never been loved like this before. No one can love like this except God. And He loves you! Again, not because *you* are good, but because *He* is. Humans who have never tasted of such a love don't know how to receive it or give it. It requires a power beyond ourselves to live in this love and walk in it every day.

And then there are those of us who *have* met God—we've asked Jesus into our heart, to be our Lord and Savior—but we're not close enough to taste of that love and to walk in it 24/7. If that's you, you can change that *today.* Who wouldn't want to be loved like that? This is a love without boundaries or conditions, a love that endures and forgives everything.

The power to love like that comes from God Himself—from the Spirit of the Lord. It comes by faith when we believe it. That's why the apostle Paul prayed this way in Ephesians 3:14-19:

> *For this reason I bow my knees to the Father of our Lord Jesus Christ, from whom the whole family in heaven and earth is named, that He*

would grant you, according to the riches of His glory, to be strengthened with might through His Spirit in the inner man, that Christ may dwell in your hearts through faith; that you, being rooted and grounded in love, may be able to comprehend with all the saints what is the width and length and depth and height—to know the love of Christ which passes knowledge; that you may be filled with all the fullness of God.

Read that verse again as if the great apostle was praying it just for you.

Nothing you have ever done or ever will do can disqualify or separate you from God's love (see Rom. 8:35). You can't be bad enough to escape this great love! God always and forever has more than enough room in His heart for you.

The day that Jesus was crucified on the Cross, there were two thieves hanging with Him, one on each side. One of them asked Jesus to remember him when He came into His kingdom, and Jesus said, *"Assuredly, I say to you, today you will be with Me in Paradise"* (Luke 23:43). That man was guilty and being justly punished for his crime, but at this very moment he is with Jesus, in the presence of joy, keeping company with Jesus and the angels, living in eternity without sadness or sickness or despair.

Our heavenly Father has a tender place in His heart for anyone who repents and turns to Him. If you've sinned and confessed your sin, He is faithful and just to forgive you and set you back on track (see 1 John 1:9). That promise is based on His faithfulness, not yours. He is faithful! He's not holding anything against you. He loves you and wants every part of you. You can trust Him with your future. You are definitely getting the better end of this deal!

You've Come a Long Way

I read a story one time that perfectly illustrates the unconditional love of God toward us. There was a little boy just learning to walk, and one day his father was trying to help him climb the stairs. He had hold of the little boy's hand and was helping, pulling him up step by step, but after about five stairs the little boy just couldn't go on.

He sat down and with all the vehemence of a toddler using his favorite word he said, "No!" The father didn't force him to continue. Instead he tousled the boy's hair and said, "That's all right, Son. You did well to come this far." Then he picked the little boy up in his arms and carried him safely the rest of the way up the stairs.

In later years, after the little boy grew up and thought about that moment, he realized that it never occurred to him that he had failed in climbing those stairs. He felt like a superstar who had conquered those five steps by himself!

That's what fathers do. They see how far you've come and they applaud you so you can learn to go the rest of the way. God wants you to know that you've come a long way, and He will help you go the rest of the way in His strength. He believes in you, and He loves you.

Proof of His Love

None of us can come into a deeper relationship with God without a revelation of His love for us—and we can't get that revelation of love without His Word. Here are seven proofs from the Bible that He loves you:

Proof Number One: Even before He lived in you, He longed to be closer to you.

Remember how under the old covenant the presence of God on earth was in the Ark of the Covenant (see Exod. 25:10-22; Lev. 16:2). Remember how the Ark was located in the Tabernacle behind the veil, and no human could approach it (except once a year) because sinful man could not approach holy God.

But when God was planning His new covenant with mankind, He wanted to reestablish the same close, loving relationship He had with Adam before sin separated them. He wanted to be so close that He planned to come live in our hearts, because we are in His heart.

He gives a glimpse of the plan in Jeremiah 24:7 when He said, *"Then I will give them a heart to know Me, that I am the Lord; and they shall be My people, and I will be their God, for they shall return to Me with their whole heart."* In Jeremiah 31:33 He said, *"I will put My law in their minds, and write it on their hearts; and I will be their God, and they shall be My people."*

When Jeremiah prophesied this message, God's people rebelled and were disobedient to Him. They were so defiant that God was about allow them to be defeated by their enemies and taken away to foreign lands as prisoners, exiled from the Promised Land of Canaan. It wasn't a happy time in Israel's history.

Yet you can hear the heart of a loving Father crying out, telling His people that there would come a time when they would be reunited in heart and mind. God declared His never-failing, unconditional love for a rebellious and disobedient people (see Jer. 31:3). He promised them that there would be a way out—and there was. Jesus was that way out.

Proof Number Two: God knew you would never deserve forgiveness, but He saved you anyway.

The Bible says that God showed how much He loves you by sending Jesus to save you when you couldn't save yourself: *"God demonstrates His own love toward us, in that while we were still sinners, Christ died for us"* (Rom. 5:8).

God knew that you would never be good enough on your own and that you could never earn your way back into fellowship with Him. You could never do enough to attain admittance to heaven. Therefore, out of His great love He sent His Son to make a way for us. He loved you first—before you were ever made righteous!

God didn't require that you prove yourself worthy; He just grabbed you into His arms despite your lost and dying condition, and then He saved you. He proved His love to you before you ever had an opportunity to do anything for Him: *"In this is love, not that we loved God, but that He loved us and sent His Son to be the propitiation for our sins"* (1 John 4:10).

God's Word makes it clear:

> *But God, who is rich in mercy, because of His great love with which He loved us, even when we were dead in trespasses, made us alive together with Christ (by grace you have been saved), and raised us up together, and made us sit together in the heavenly places in Christ Jesus, that in the ages to come He might show the exceeding riches of His grace in His kindness toward us in Christ Jesus* (Ephesians 2:4-7).

God wants to show off in you, not because of anything you've done (or haven't done), but because of His great mercy and His great love for you.

Proof Number Three: He gave to you.

God didn't just shout down from heaven, "I love you!" No, instead He sent His Son. He committed Himself to you, in the flesh. First John 4:9 says, *"This is how God showed his love for us: God sent his only Son into the world so we might live through him"* (MSG).

Sometimes people feel as if God is holding back from them, thinking that He could do more to help them or answer their prayers. By sending Jesus, God gave His best for you. He didn't hold anything back!

Romans 8:32 says, *"He who did not spare His own Son, but delivered Him up for us all, how shall He not with Him also freely give us all things?"*

If God was going to hold anything back from you, it would have been His precious Son. I have sons. I've tried on this idea in my head: Could I give my son for you (or for anyone)? That would be a sacrifice! In giving Jesus, God has proven beyond any doubt that He will freely give you anything. He loves you. Don't doubt it or question it.

Proof Number Four: God thinks you're the most valuable thing on earth.

It is said that the value of something is determined by the price that was paid for it. Think of an auction. If a ring sells for one thousand dollars in one round, but a necklace goes for ten thousand dollars in the next round, we would say that the necklace is *more valuable* because the higher price was paid for it.

Following this logic, you can conclude that *humans* must be the most valuable things on the planet, because the highest price was paid for them—the precious blood of God's Son.

The Bible says, *"You were not redeemed with corruptible things, like silver or gold…but with the precious blood of Christ, as of a lamb without blemish and without spot"* (1 Pet. 1:18-19).

Notice that God calls silver and gold "corruptible," meaning something that could disintegrate or become tainted. That is *not* what I think of when I think of silver or gold. Do you?

If I were to come to your house with two suitcases, one full of silver and the other full of gold, and open them in your living room, you probably wouldn't look in and say, "Ah, corruptible." No, you'd probably say, "May I have some?" Because you would look at the silver and gold and think, "*Valuable!*"

By contrast, God said He needed something *more* precious (valuable) than gold or silver to buy you, because *you* are the most valuable thing to Him. He needed something that would never change, disintegrate, or decrease in value. And there was only one thing that met those requirements—the blood of His only Son.

Don't believe the lies of the devil when he says you're not worth much. The highest price was paid for you.

Proof Number Five: God hears you.

I'm sure there have been times in your life when you've felt that God wasn't being very attentive to you. Maybe you've felt like you were praying but He wasn't listening. But the Bible disproves that. It says that when you talk, He is listening.

Psalm 40:1 says, *"I waited patiently for the Lord; and He inclined to me, and heard my cry."* When I read the word *inclined*, I picture God leaning over from His throne to listen. He hears me. He always hears when I cry out to Him. And He hears you too. Psalm 34:4 says, *"I sought the Lord, and He heard me, and delivered me from all my fears."*

Does it matter that God hears you? I think it makes all the difference. If He didn't hear you when you called out to Him, how could He deliver you from all of your fears? If you call a company's customer service number and get transferred from recording to recording until you hang up in frustration, you end the call knowing that no one at the company heard you. That is *not* a satisfactory phone call.

There are people who feel as if God is like that customer service call—that He doesn't hear them when they pray. What a hopeless feeling that must be. But that is not what the Bible says about prayer or God; rather, it says He hears you! And that makes all the difference. First John 5:14-15 says, *"Now this is the confidence that we have in Him, that if we ask anything according to His will, He hears us. And if we know that He hears us, whatever we ask, we know that we have the petitions that we have asked of Him."*

Knowing that God hears you gives you confidence that your prayer is being answered. If you thought He wasn't listening, you would never be able to believe. In fact, you would conclude that it is fruitless to talk with Him. That would be true hopelessness. But, fear not, God repeatedly promises in His Word that He is listening.

Proof Number Six: You are God's personal concern.

There are a lot of scriptures that say God doesn't want you to worry or be anxious or afraid about anything. He tells you in 1 Peter 5:7 to cast every care on Him, because He cares so much for you. The J.B. Phillips version translates 1 Peter 5:7: *"You can throw the whole weight of your anxieties upon him, for you are his personal concern."*

Think about that. You are God's personal concern! I liken it to the President. Every person in America is the President's concern, yet most of us don't have his personal cell number or the access to reach him anytime, do we? We are his constituents, and while he is concerned about us in the general sense, we aren't his *personal* concern.

But I'll bet his family members have his cell number or can reach him anytime they need to. That's because they are his personal concern! He is personally responsible for them in a way that he isn't for us. If his kids are in the hospital, he's responsible to visit them and pay their bill. If you or I are in the hospital, there will probably be no visit, and he won't personally pay our bill.

A lot of Christians look at themselves as God's constituent, not as His child. Like, yes, He's up there, He cares about me in a general sense, but not deeply. But that's not true—you are His *personal* concern! He is your Father. That puts things in a whole different light.

When it comes to solving your problems, God doesn't look at you as just another item on His to-do list. In reality, He gives you personal attention, because you're a member of His family. A father is responsible for members of his family in a way that he's not responsible for his associates or neighbors.

Proof Number Seven: You have access.

As we talked about in Chapter 3, the veil between man and God has been removed by the blood of Jesus. Hebrews 4:16 says, *"Let us therefore come boldly to the throne of grace, that we may obtain mercy and find grace to help in time of need."* You don't have to crawl on your belly into the presence of God; rather, He tells you to come *boldly* because you have access right into His throne room. You'll never be shut out or turned away. You are completely accepted in the beloved (see Eph. 1:6).

The access you now have to God reminds me of a scene in the movie *Anna and the King.* This film tells the story of a widowed British woman, Anna, who taught school many years ago in Siam (now Thailand) to the king's children. One day during class, a fight broke out between Anna's son and the king's oldest son, the heir to the throne. The king's youngest and favorite child, a little girl about five years old, ran from the classroom to tell her father (the king) about the fight.

The king was in his throne room, meeting with hundreds of the leaders of his nation. These important governors and senators were all lined up in rows, bowing down to the king, their faces to the floor. None of them would dare approach the mighty king without being invited, on penalty of death.

When the little princess entered the huge room, she ignored these important men completely, scampering down the aisle right past them. She jumped onto the platform and hurled herself into the king's lap, saying, "Papa, Papa, guess what's happening in the school room?"

Did the king call for his guards to haul her away or behead her? Of course not, even though he would have done that if anyone else tried to approach him without permission. Instead, he listened patiently to his little daughter's breathless story about the fight, then took her hand and walked with her back down the aisle toward the classroom, leaving all of the assembled dignitaries with their faces to the floor.

That little princess came boldly to the throne because she knew she had access. She was her father's favorite, and had no fear of approaching him when she needed him.

This scene paints a perfect picture of you and your heavenly Father. You are completely accepted and loved by Him. You can approach the throne and hurl yourself into His lap anytime you want! You have access, and He loves you.

The Bible has even more proofs of your Father's perfect love for you. I have included these seven to help get you started, and to give you a *knowing* that you are loved. I encourage you to bathe your spirit in these truths. That is the way to *know and believe* the love that God has for you.

Review in a Nutshell

God loves you with an everlasting love—you have never been loved like this before. When you believe that, it will draw you closer to Him and change your life.

Now Engage:

Read and meditate the scriptures we've looked at, and activate the power of God's Word in your life by speaking these declarations out loud.

> *And we have known and believed the love that God has for us. God is love, and he who abides in love abides in God, and God in him* (1 John 4:16).

Declare:

> "God loves me! I've never been loved like this before. I abide with Him and get close to Him by believing the love He has for me. I believe that the entire intent of His heart toward me is good—everything He does is born out of His love."

> *Beloved, let us love one another, for love is of God; and everyone who loves is born of God and knows God. He who does not love does not know God, for God is love* (1 John 4:7-8).

Declare:

> "God doesn't just *have* love—He *is* love. He is the very essence of love—His whole being is love. That means His entire motivation toward me is love. He is the lover of my soul."

> *As the deer pants for the water brooks, so pants my soul for You, O God* (Psalm 42:1).

Declare:

> "I was created to love God and to fellowship with Him. Like every person, there's a place inside me that only He can fill. My soul craves fellowship and closeness with my Creator. I won't try to fill the void with anything else. I will pursue my relationship with the One who created me."

> *And we have known and believed the love that God has for us* (1 John 4:16).

Declare:

> "God loves me because He is love, not because I'm so loveable. He loves me because *He* is good, not because I am. I can't earn and deserve this love—I can only receive it and believe it. God knows everything about me— the good, the bad, and the ugly—and He loves me unconditionally."

For the grace of God that brings salvation has appeared to all men, teaching us that, denying ungodliness and worldly lusts, we should live soberly, righteously, and godly in the present age (Titus 2:11-12).

Declare:

"I am empowered from within by God's grace to withstand temptation and walk in a way that honors and pleases Him. I don't use grace as an excuse to sin. Instead, grace helps me to deny ungodliness and lust so I can live soberly, righteously, and godly. I can't do it on my own, but God's given me His grace to do it."

Behold, the days are coming, says the Lord, when I will make a new covenant with the house of Israel and with the house of Judah...I will put My law in their minds, and write it on their hearts; and I will be their God, and they shall be My people (Jeremiah 31:31,33).

Declare:

"God wants my heart. He did everything in His power to bring me back to His heart—He sent Jesus. All He wants from me in return is to believe what He's done through Jesus and to love Him with all *my heart*. Loving and serving God is what I do in response to His love. I love Him, and I live to please Him."

God demonstrates His own love toward us, in that while we were still sinners, Christ died for us (Romans 5:8).

Declare:

"God showed how much He loves me by sending Jesus to save me when I couldn't save myself or earn my way back into fellowship with Him. He loved me first. He didn't require that I prove myself worthy; He just grabbed me into His arms and saved me. He proved His love to me before I ever had an opportunity to do anything for Him."

He who did not spare His own Son, but delivered Him up for us all, how shall He not with Him also freely give us all things?" (Romans 8:32)

Declare:

"God is not holding anything back from me. In giving Jesus, God has proven beyond any doubt that He will freely give me anything. He loves me. I don't doubt it or question it."

You were not redeemed with corruptible things, like silver or gold…but with the precious blood of Christ, as of a lamb without blemish and without spot (1 Peter 1:18-19).

Declare:

> "God used something more precious than gold
> or silver to buy me, because I am the most valu-
> able thing to Him. He needed something that
> would never change, disintegrate, or decrease
> in value. And there was only one thing that
> met those requirements—the blood of His
> only Son. I am the most valuable thing to God,
> because the highest price was paid for me."

> *I sought the Lord, and He heard me, and deliv-*
> *ered me from all my fears. ...I waited patiently*
> *for the Lord; and He inclined to me, and heard*
> *my cry* (Psalm 34:4; 40:1).

Declare:

> "When I talk to God, I know that He hears
> me. The Bible says He leans over from His
> throne to listen to me. Knowing that God
> hears me gives me confidence that my prayers
> are being answered."

> *You can throw the whole weight of your anxiet-*
> *ies upon him, for you are his personal concern* (1
> Peter 5:7 PHILLIPS).

Declare:

> "I am God's personal concern. He is my Father,
> and a father is responsible for members of his
> family in a way that he's not responsible for

his associates or neighbors. God doesn't look at me as just another item on His to-do list—He gives me personal attention, because I'm a member of His family."

Let us therefore come boldly to the throne of grace, that we may obtain mercy and find grace to help in time of need (Hebrews 4:16).

Declare:

"I can come boldly to God any time because I have access. I don't have to crawl on my belly into His presence. I'll never be shut out or turned away—I'm completely accepted and loved by Him."

Discussion Questions:

Has this chapter helped you to better understand how much God loves you? Do you feel like God has your whole heart, or are there parts of yourself you withhold from Him? What happened when you tried the test on page 99?

Chapter Five

GOD'S HEART

IT'S SO IMPORTANT TO REALIZE HOW MUCH GOD LOVES US, because it undergirds our very lives as Christians. And just as important, this is the love that you and I are supposed to show the world—the love that draws others to salvation and a relationship with God.

In order to walk closer than we ever imagined with God, we have to love what He loves—and He loves people. The more we understand His love for us, the more we can love people the way He does—we can love them with His love. That's the kind of love we described in the last chapter.

That's really what we are on earth to do—fellowship with God and declare the Good News of His love to people so they can be saved (see 1 Tim. 2:4). This is how we bring in the great last-days harvest before Jesus returns.

Putting the Other Person First

So what does walking in this God-kind of love look like? In a nutshell, this love does what's better for the other person. It puts the other person first. That's what Jesus did for us. In the Garden of Gethsemane when He saw clearly the sacrifice that He was going to have to make on the Cross, He asked God if that cup could pass from Him. *The Message* says that Jesus "*fell on his face, praying, 'My Father, if there is any way, get me out of this. But please, not what I want. You, what do you want?'*" (Matt. 26:39 MSG). His own choice would have been to not go through that.

But He didn't put His own wishes first—He put you and me first. He said to the Father, who had been planning this great redemption for 4,000 years: "Not my will, but your will be done." That is the picture of love. In spite of the pain, the shame, the separation from God that He would endure, He did what was best for us. He went to the Cross and shed His blood, paying the ultimate price, making the ultimate sacrifice.

John 15:13 says, "*Greater love has no one than this, than to lay down one's life for his friends.*" This is the kind of love that God put in our hearts when we were born again, and that's the kind of love you and I are called to walk in. Jesus is our example. He gave Himself first.

What if everyone who is married did this with their spouse? What if we did it with our children, our co-workers, our fellow students, our neighbors, or other family members? What if, when we're dealing with a difficult person, we chose to walk in love instead of getting even or wanting them to change? I think we'd find a whole lot more of God's power applied to our situations, and we'd come out on top every time.

Jesus Showed Us How

When I consider that Jesus gave His all for me, it doesn't seem impossible to give my all for Him. He showed me how. He made a way for us all when there was no way—a way of escape from sin, a way back to the Father, a way to walk worthy of Him. In gratitude for all He's done for me, I want to do the same for Him—to imitate Him and walk in that same kind of selfless, liberating love that He does.

That's why Ephesians 5:1-2 says we can only walk in love with others by imitating what God Himself has done for us and in us:

> *Therefore be imitators of God as dear children.*
> *And walk in love, as Christ also has loved us and*
> *given Himself for us, an offering and a sacrifice*
> *to God for a sweet-smelling aroma.*

The Bible tells us that the first commandment is to love God with all our hearts, and then second is to "*love your neighbor as yourself*" (Mark 12:30-31). First of all, how can you love your neighbor if you don't love yourself? You have to know who you are and how much God loves you. Second, it's much easier to love your neighbor when you know you're not doing it on your own—you're doing with the love of God that is in you (see Rom. 5:5).

The Struggle Is Real

Sometimes when I encourage people to walk in love, it isn't always well-received. Somehow, as soon as I say, "Walk in love"—either from the pulpit or across a counseling desk, or even to a friend—people get a distasteful look on their face, kind of like they just ate a lemon.

Let's be real—we struggle with walking in love. I think maybe we think, "If I walk in love with them, they're going to get their way and I'm not going to get mine." We can identify with Peter in Matthew 18:21 who said to Jesus, *"Lord, how often shall my brother sin against me, and I forgive him? Up to seven times?"* Peter was using all his faith here— he thought forgiving seven times sounded pretty spiritual!

Imagine his surprise when Jesus answered, *"I do not say to you, up to seven times, but up to seventy times seven"* (Matt. 18:22). That sounded impossible to Peter! And I don't even think Jesus meant that once you'd forgiven someone 490 times, it was okay to hold a grudge. I think He was saying, "Every time, Peter."

Why would Jesus set such a high mark that seemed almost impossible? Because He knows that forgiveness is freedom. He knows that unforgiveness is like drinking poison and expecting the other person to die—it eats us alive. It's bondage. (You can read more about how to walk in forgiveness in my book *I Forgive You, But….*)

Peter was probably thinking, "No way, Lord." Just like most of the people think when I talk to them about walking in love. Let's face it—it's not humanly possible to forgive or walk in love at that level.

And here's the thing: he was right. It *isn't* humanly possible. But with God, all things are possible (see Matt. 19:26).

When you know God's heart for people and how He has put His love inside you, then we can tap into *His* power to love and forgive even the toughest person.

Believing the Love

I like the way one friend of mine puts it: *Love isn't what you do, it's what you receive.* First John 4:10 says, *"In this is love, not that we loved God, but that He loved us."* Love is always God's top priority—both *for* you and *through* you. You may have often heard in church that you should love God, but God says, "I love *you!*" He started it. And when you believe it, it changes your life. Then with that love, you can love others.

We've talked a lot about the believing the love God has for you, and that's also the answer for walking in love. Proverbs 23:7 says that as a man thinks in his heart, so will he be. What you believe in your heart will be reflected in your life. If you struggle with believing that God loves you and has forgiven you in Christ, then walking in love and forgiving people will be hard for you.

The best thing to do if you struggle with walking in love or forgiving is to press into God's love for you. Study about it. Read 1 John a lot. Ask God to help you see His love for you more clearly every day. He'll be happy to oblige!

Just like Peter, our ability to walk in love or forgive is limited when we try to do it in our own strength—by our own feelings or understanding. We can't be the source of this kind of love. But when we believe that God's love is in us—when we connect to the love God has for us and the forgiveness He applies to us—then we have a limitless supply of love and forgiveness that can flow through us.

When I think about *how good* God has been to me—how generous, and loving, and forgiving—and how the greatness of His power is toward me to answer every prayer and take care of every problem (see Eph. 1:19), it just makes me want to share that love with everyone, even difficult people.

And I've found that when I approach people with that attitude, something wonderful happens. It's hard to describe, because it's supernatural, but I can almost say it's like the surrounding atmosphere becomes "softer." When I approach someone with the love of God as the top priority in my mind, it smooths things out and causes people to be more receptive—both to me and to the Gospel.

It all comes from being closer to Him, believing He loves me, and walking with Him every day. First John 4:8 says, *"He who does not love does not know God, for God is love."* I think we can say that the other way too: "He (or she) who knows God, loves!" Loving should be as natural to a Christian as breathing. When you know and believe you're loved by God, it just flows out of you, and then the world can see what Jesus said in John 13:35—they will know us by our love.

Review in a Nutshell

Getting closer to God means loving what He loves—and He loves people. The more we understand His love for us, the more we can walk in love with people the way He does and draw them to salvation and a relationship with God.

Now Engage:

Read and meditate the scriptures we've looked at, and activate the power of God's Word in your life by speaking these declarations out loud.

> [God] *desires all men to be saved and to come to the knowledge of the truth* (1 Timothy 2:4).

Declare:

> "In order to walk closer with God, I will love what He loves—and He loves people. The more I understand His love for me, the more I can love people the way He does—I can love them with His love. That's what I'm on earth to do—fellowship with God and declare the Good News of His love to people so they can be saved."

> *Greater love has no one than this, than to lay down one's life for his friends* (John 15:13).

Declare:

> "Jesus laid down His life for me, and that's the kind of love God put in my heart when I was born again. That's the kind of love I am called to walk in—love that does what's better for the other person. Jesus is my example. I will walk in love like Jesus did."

> *Therefore be imitators of God as dear children. And walk in love, as Christ also has loved us and given Himself for us, an offering and a sacrifice to God for a sweet-smelling aroma* (Ephesians 5:1-2).

Declare:

> "When I consider that Jesus gave His all for me, it doesn't seem impossible to give my all for Him. He showed me how. He made a way of escape from sin; a way back to the Father; a way to walk worthy of Him. In gratitude for all He's done for me, I want to imitate Him and walk in that same kind of selfless, liberating love that He does."

> *"Lord, how often shall my brother sin against me, and I forgive him? Up to seven times?" Jesus said to him, "I do not say to you, up to seven times, but up to seventy times seven"* (Matthew 18:21-22).

Declare:

> "It sounds impossible to forgive someone 490 times a day, but Jesus knows that forgiveness is freedom. It's *not* humanly possible to forgive or walk in love at that level, but with God all things are possible. I know God's heart for people, and how He has put His love inside me, so I will tap into *His* power to love and forgive even the toughest person."

In this is love, not that we loved God, but that He loved us (1 John 4:10)

Declare:

> "Love is always God's top priority—both *for* me and *through* me. He started it. I can't be the source of this kind of love. But I believe that God's love is in me and I connect to the love God has for me and the forgiveness He applies to me. That gives me a limitless supply of love and forgiveness that can flow through me."

He who does not love does not know God, for God is love (1 John 4:8).

By this all will know that you are My disciples, if you have love for one another (John 13:35).

Declare:

> "Loving is as natural to me as breathing because I know and believe the love God has for me.

When I think about how good God has been to me—how generous and loving and forgiving—and how He's answered my prayers and taken care of my problems, it makes me want to share that love with everyone, even difficult people."

Discussion Questions:

Have you had trouble walking in love with people? Is it hard for you to forgive? Do you think it's important for us to show God's love to the world?

Chapter Six

QUALITY TIME

LET ME ASK YOU A QUESTION: HOW DID YOU GET CLOSE TO the people you're close to? How did you get to know your parents, your best friend, your love, as well as you do? The answer is, you talked to them. You spent quality time with them. You listened to them and shared your heart with them. You couldn't wait to hang out with them—it hasn't been a burden to get closer and closer to them, it's been a joy!

That's the same way you'll get to know God in a deeper, more intimate way. Intimacy is built in all the little moments when you are just spending time together. As I've said before, many people know *about* God. But we'll only truly know Him deeply—walk freely in His presence, be able to trust Him in every circumstance, and have His power flowing to and through our life—when we've spent quality time with Him. It's not a burden—it's a joy.

Be Still

There is so much vying for our attention in today's "information age." A tidal wave of data and information washes over us every day. We're inundated with news, images, emails, notifications, alerts, and more. Computers and smart phones have revolutionized the way we create, store, and retrieve information on a whim. A global economy and instant communication have created an explosion of data that we are exposed to every day.

The average adult consumes five times more information every day than the average adult did 50 years ago. Our brains are working overtime to process and filter all the data, trying to determine what is and *isn't* important to our survival. There's more data available than we can ever possibly process. Scientists are saying that the overwhelming amount of information invading our thoughts day after day is affecting our minds and can lead to agitation, confusion, and decision paralysis.

We're getting so much information that it's hard to quiet our minds down enough to focus on one thing at a time.

That can sound depressing, but I truly believe that God knew exactly what you and I would be dealing with in the 21st century. He put us on earth for such a time as this, and He's not surprised or worried by the technology we live with. I believe He has absolutely given us the wisdom and the grace to deal with it and use it to our best advantage.

But it's up to us to tap into that wisdom on a daily basis! I believe it's the most crucial thing that you and I must discipline ourselves to do. And it's the only way to develop a deeper relationship with our Heavenly Father.

Psalm 46:10, although written centuries ago, is completely applicable for today and gives us a huge key in how to overcome the mind-numbing flow of worldly information and be intimately and securely anchored in our relationship with our Father. It says, *"Be still, and know that I am God."*

That is a loaded admonition, isn't it? In today's fast-paced, highly driven, stressed-out world, we are not very good at being still. Yet this verse shows us that if we *will* be still, we can know God. And when you know God, you have every advantage. I would venture to say, with all that's going on around us every day, we *need* to be still. When we're still, we are simply in a better position to hear from God.

Charge Up!

God made us in such a way that we need this recharging every day. Let me use your cell phone as an analogy. Your cell phone won't go forever without being plugged into a power source on a regular basis. You have to charge that puppy up at least once a day if you want to keep using it, right?

What happens if you forget to charge it—if you just get too busy and don't have time to plug it in? It's going to die on you. And without power, that phone is useless to you.

You are the same way. You can't go forever without plugging into *your* power source, which is God. If you want to keep operating effectively—hearing His voice, walking in His plan, resisting the enemy, maintaining your joy, peace, and prosperity—you have to charge up at least once a day by reading and meditating on your Bible, praying, and spending quality time with your Creator. It's the only way to stay close to Him.

If you get too busy or don't have time to plug in, what's going to happen? You won't exactly die, but you won't be sharp, either. You'll be easily confused or tempted, you'll be stressed and frazzled, you'll lose sight of your life's goals, you'll get in trouble financially, and a myriad of other things.

Have you ever had that feeling that you *need* something? And you kind of wander around looking for it (usually in the fridge, or the phone, or...). Too many times we try to fill that *need* with things like eating, binge watching, sports, social media, or even drugs and alcohol to numb the pain.

But it's really our hearts crying out for more of God! Only He can fill that void in our soul. And when we draw near to Him, He draws near to us and willingly pours into us His love, His wisdom, His help (see James 4:8). Every time He does that, we come to know Him more. But we are the ones who must approach first. Then He's right there to give us everything we need.

Without God's power flowing to you and through you every day, you're on your own. And we all know how that works out. I like to say it this way: every day you go without reading your Bible is a day you're trying to live life in your own strength and *it's too hard for you!*

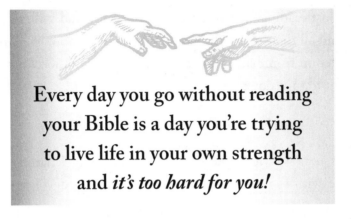

Every day you go without reading your Bible is a day you're trying to live life in your own strength and *it's too hard for you!*

God has given us His Word so we can know His will. It's meant to be used as a sword to do battle with every negative situation in our life and bring us through to victory (see Eph. 6:17). He's given us an open invitation, 24/7, to come and spend time in His presence. To tell Him our worries and leave them in His capable hands. To get His wisdom and perspective on problems. To refuel, reboot, and renew our souls. Jesus tells us:

> *Come to Me, all who are weary and burdened, and I will give you rest. Put My yoke upon your shoulders—it might appear heavy at first, but it is perfectly fitted to your curves. Learn from Me, for I am gentle and humble of heart. When you are yoked to Me, your weary souls will find*

rest. *For My yoke is easy, and My burden is light* (Matthew 11:28-30 VOICE).

What a promise! I don't know about you, but I feel better just reading that scripture. He is ready and willing to spend all the time in the world with us. He knows we'll be better off from having done it. That is an invitation I never want to turn down.

Daily Devotions

The best way to make sure you spend daily "charge up" time with God is to develop a habit of daily devotions. I like to meet with God early in the morning, simply because it gives me a good start to my day when the house is still quiet and nothing is clamoring for my attention.

I love to "fill up" with God and lay my day out before Him so He can guide and help me every step of the way. If you're more a night person than a morning person, it's totally okay to do your devotions in the evening if that works better for you.

My best advice is to make an appointment with yourself for your devotional time, and don't let anything interrupt or shanghai you. Because something will always try! Have you ever settled down to read the Bible or pray, and the phone rings? Or the kids cry? Or you think of something you need at the grocery store? Yeah, me too.

We have to discipline ourselves to focus in on this daily time with God and make it a habit that we do automatically. Think of it like an appointment with a physician or beautician that you had to wait a long time to get into. You'll move heaven and earth to keep that appointment. Get that same attitude about keeping your daily appointment with God.

Because everything changes in the presence of God (see Ps. 119:130). A daily devotional time gives you opportunity to be still enough in your soul to receive all that He is, all that He has for you.

> *It is good to give thanks to the Lord, and to sing praises to Your name, O Most High; to declare Your lovingkindness in the morning, and Your faithfulness every night* (Psalm 92:1-2).

I promise you that setting aside this daily time to spend with God will be well worth it. And it's really the way you'll get to know Him better, walking in that close intimacy that He wants and you crave.

Do whatever you can to carve out this wonderful, personal time with God. Get up a little earlier if you have to. I can't overemphasize the importance of this time you spend with God. Everything hinges on it. It's not a duty—it's a joy!

Here's an example of things I do in my daily devotional time with God:

1. Praise and give thanks

2. Read the Bible

3. Pray

4. Pray in the Spirit

5. Make the day's schedule

This is not a hard and fast "schedule" by any means—you do what works for you. These are just meant to give you some ideas of how you can spend your time with Him.

#1 Praise and Give Thanks

I like to start out my time with God by praising Him and thanking Him for all He's done for me. It puts me in the right frame of mind—a frame of fellowship, not just asking. Some people only think of approaching God when they need something. They think of approaching God as a time when they express all their needs to Him, asking for His help.

Yes, we have needs, and yes, God wants to hear about them and help us—absolutely! But need is not what builds a relationship. What if you had a friend who only wanted to talk to you when they needed something? That would not be a very good friendship!

Remember, God wants your heart, not just your prayer requests. He wants to be close to you. He wants to share things with you. And it does your heart good when you acknowledge all He's done for you and come to Him with a grateful and thankful attitude.

It's easy to do, really. Isn't He worthy of all our praise? Hasn't He been good to us? He's so worthy and so good! He's done so much for us! He's saved us, healed us, bought us back from death and hell, made every provision for us, given us His love, His peace, and His joy. He's made a home for us with Himself in heaven where we'll live forever, ruling and reigning with Him! Not only that, but He's always paying attention to every minute detail of your life, working all things together for your good when you ask Him to (see Rom. 8:28).

I could go on and on—you get the point. If you have trouble thanking God for all His benefits and all He's done for you, just start with those I've listed. Meditate on these verses and how they apply in your life:

> *Oh, give thanks to the Lord, for He is good! For His mercy endures forever* (Psalm 107:1).
>
> *In everything give thanks; for this is the will of God in Christ Jesus for you* (1 Thessalonians 5:18).
>
> *Continue earnestly in prayer, being vigilant in it with thanksgiving* (Colossians 4:2).
>
> *Enter his gates with thanksgiving, and his courts with praise! Give thanks to him; bless his name! For the Lord is good; his steadfast love endures forever, and his faithfulness to all generations* (Psalm 100:4-5 ESV).
>
> *Give thanks to the Lord, for he is good; his love endures forever* (Psalm 118:29 NIV).
>
> *I will give thanks to you, Lord, with all my heart; I will tell of all your wonderful deeds* (Psalm 9:1 NIV).

> *Therefore by Him let us continually offer the sacrifice of praise to God, that is, the fruit of our lips, giving thanks to His name* (Hebrews 13:15).

Yes, there are days in everyone's life when it seems hard to thank and praise God—days when it really *is* a sacrifice (see Heb. 13:15). Days when you're struggling or feeling down. Maybe you're tired, or it just seems like God has let you down or just doesn't seem care about your troubles. Maybe something terrible has happened, and you're reeling from the pain of it.

I understand those days—I've been there too. When my first husband died so suddenly at age 37, I felt completely lost, not knowing what to do next—I was numb. I know what it feels like to have the bottom fall out of your world.

But here's what I learned. Every day, you and I have a choice to thank God. No matter how dark it looks, there is always something to thank Him for. And once you start, something happens in your heart and you start to realize that no matter what you face, God is working. Praise releases the supernatural power of God. When you praise Him, you start to have hope, and then faith, that you're going to come out on top.

A Miracle Story of Praise

Miracles happen and we praise God. I once heard a story about a woman missionary in China many years ago. She contracted a deadly disease and was given up to die.

For days she lay quarantined in her bunk, with no medical help—it was a hopeless situation.

The only thing she could do was pray. So hour after hour, she pled with God to heal her. Then suddenly the Lord gave her a vision. She saw an old-fashioned scale, the kind often seen on justice statues, with a fulcrum and plates held by chains on each side. This scale she saw was heavily weighted on one side, while the other side was way up in the air because it was empty. The scale was clearly out of balance.

The Lord revealed to her that the heavy side was her prayers—she had certainly prayed many prayers—while the empty side was her praise. God quickened to her that the praise side needed to be filled to outweigh the trouble she was facing. When the scale was balanced, her healing would be manifested.

So this desperately sick woman stopped pleading for her healing and started praising God. She praised Him for His greatness. She praised Him for sending Jesus and for all His benefits. She praised Him for being her Savior, her healer, her provider, and for everything He'd ever done for her.

At first, she was so weak that her praises were mere whispers. But as she continued to do nothing but praise and worship God all day and all night, she grew louder. As the people outside her room heard her fervent praises they feared for her life, thinking that maybe she was delirious with fever. You can imagine how amazed they were, several days later, when she walked out of that room on her own, totally healed! She had taken "the praise cure" and she was completely made well.

There is power in praise! When we shift our focus from our troubles to God's greatness, miracles can happen.

Five Benefits of Praise

1. Praising and giving thanks helps you to magnify God (see Ps. 34:3) and get your focus back on Him. Dwelling on your troubles makes you prisoner to them, but dwelling on God makes Him bigger than all the problems and pains.

2. Praising God keeps you humble. Praising and thanking God reminds you that you are dependent on Him—you're not in this alone, you need Him.

3. When you're humble, you get more grace (see James 4:6), and grace is God's power beyond your ability, working to bring you through every trouble in your life.

4. Praising helps your brain when you think of all that you have to be thankful for, even the little things.

5. Praising stirs up your faith. When you praise and worship God, you're reminded afresh that He is your provider, your healer, your

help, your strength, and whatever else you need. He is working (see Rom. 8:28)!

As you start your daily devotional time let your heart and soul soar to Him in praise.

#2 Read the Bible

The Bible is God talking to you. It's where you find out who you are and how to live a life of victory. In a world that's constantly changing, constantly confusing, and very often wrong, the Bible is your anchor—the very foundation of your life. God has said, *"Heaven and earth will pass away, but My words will by no means pass away"* (Matt. 24:35). He says He has exalted His Word above His Name (see Ps. 138:2), and His Word will never return void but will always accomplish what He sent it to do (see Isa. 55:11).

You and I need God's Word in our life! There's no way to live the supernatural kind of life that Jesus died to give us or get to know Him intimately without reading His Word. His Word is His will for us. We can't separate God from His Word.

Too many Christians view reading the Bible as a duty or some sort of dry activity that they "must do" in order to be "good Christians" or in order to receive God's blessings. But that's not why we read it. First of all, we don't read it to get the blessings—it's too late! We've already received all God's blessings in Christ (see Eph. 1:3)!

No, we read the Bible to see what those blessings are, and to keep them in the forefront of our mind so we can contend for them in everyday life. We read it so we know what belongs to us—so we have the faith to say, "No devil! That's not in my covenant; I resist you in Jesus' Name!" We read the Bible to hear God's voice and follow His path for our lives. I call it "God's Instruction Manual for Life." It's vital to read the instructions!

Nine Reasons to Read Your Bible Every Day

1. **It has your answers**. John 14:27 says you can hear His voice and follow Him. The Bible is how you learn to recognize God's voice, get His guidance, and make right decisions.

2. **Faith comes by hearing the Word of God** (see Rom. 10:17), and all of God's blessings come by faith (by believing that what He has said is true). First John 5:4 says, *"**This** is the victory that has overcome the world—our faith."* Faith comes by hearing, and it's developed by using. Faith is crucial to your life, and it comes from the Bible.

3. **It tells you how to live the God-kind of life**. John 10:10 says that Jesus came to give you the God-kind of abundant life. Read in His Word about how to live life like He lives it. He's never worried, never broke, never sick. That's the kind of life He wants you to live.

4. **It's how you see who you are**—and what needs changing. James 1:22-25 says the Word is like a mirror. It solidifies who you are (the

righteousness of God in Christ) in your heart and mind, and like any mirror it also helps you see things that need changing. I'm so thankful that His Word points out things I'm not doing correctly so I can change and keep growing up in Him (see Eph. 4:14-15).

5. **It's where the power is**. Romans 1:16 says the gospel is the power of God unto salvation. That word "salvation" is *sozo*, which means deliverance, safety, preservation, healing, soundness. When you know what belongs to you from reading in the Word, you can contend for your covenant blessings and expect the power of God to work in you and through you.

6. **It's how to *know* God**. As you read His Word you see how He thinks, how He moves, how He loves you. You are reading God's story, getting to know how He acts in situations, how He feels toward you. You can't get closer to God without reading His Word.

7. **The Word of God is our only offensive weapon against the enemy** (see Eph. 6:17). We are meant to read it, hide it in our hearts, and speak it out our mouths when we face fears, troubles and setbacks. *"Since we have the same spirit of faith, according to what is written, 'I believed and therefore I spoke,' we also believe*

and therefore speak" (2 Cor. 4:13). You can only use it as a weapon if you've been reading it.

8. **It will help you overcome in the midst of
   tough times**. When my first husband died
   suddenly, I clung to the Word. I read it for
   hours every day—I knew I had to have it. It's
   how I not only survived, but thrived during
   the hardest time of my life.

9. **It's how you win over the enemy**. Mark 4:15
   tells us that Satan comes to steal the Word
   from us. That's because he knows that a
   Christian with the Word hidden in our heart
   and spoken out our mouth is so dangerous to
   his kingdom!

There are so many benefits to reading God's Word
that I could go on and on about it! It is the source of our
strength, it's how we tap into the wisdom of the ages, it's
how we learn to hear God's voice and receive His guidance,
it's how we have confidence in Him and how our families
can live a life of blessings in Him.

What Keeps You from Reading the Bible?

Not long ago, I did an informal survey on social media
and asked people, "What keeps you from reading the
Bible?" I got some real, transparent, everyday-life kinds of
answers from people who were really struggling with reading the Bible.

Lots of people said things like procrastination, distractions, laziness, wasting time (like on social media), wrong priorities, poor time management. Here were a few specific reasons they gave—maybe you can identify:

- "Letting other things that seem more pressing take my focus and time."

- "Saying I'll read it later, and the next thing I know the day is over."

- "There's just not enough time in a day—I'm too busy."

- "I don't get enough sleep! Every time I try to read the Bible, I fall asleep."

- "I have never been a reader. I always hated to read."

- "Sometimes I just don't feel like reading the Bible."

- "I don't know where to start. I'm intimidated by the material and knowing where to focus my attention."

- "I haven't seen any good results from reading the Bible—I'm disappointed. It's hard to read something that isn't working for me."

- "It's kind of a downward spiral...the less I read my Bible the less I want to."

Do any of those sound familiar? If so, what can you do to stop the "downward spiral" and make daily Bible reading a daily habit so it can empower your life? Here are some practical tips:

1—Keep Going

Listen, I get it. We all want answers and manifestations *now*, and if that doesn't happen, disappointment can set in. But here's the deal—*stopping* is not going to get you there! Be honest about your disappointment, tell God about it, then *keep going*.

The good news is that the more you read the Bible, the more you want to! I heard someone say it this way: What you give yourself to, you create a desire for. Isn't that the truth? It's like binge-watching Netflix—the more you watch, the more you want to watch!

I remember when my first husband Brent started learning to play golf. His uncle was determined to teach him, but he hated it. Every time they had a golf date, Brent wanted to cancel. But his uncle persevered, and after a few weeks of regular play, Brent started loving it. Why? The more he played, the more he wanted to. It works that way with Bible-reading too.

It's like going to the gym. You might not feel like going. You might come up with all sorts of "busy" excuses to put it off—you just don't *feel* like carving out the extra time or putting forth the effort.

But then a few months later, you don't like how you look or feel—you're all doughy and out of shape! The same thing happens after long periods of not reading God's

Word—you can easily get out of shape spiritually. Then the devil can run rampant over your life!

You usually don't see the result right away of skipping the gym—it takes some time—and you don't see the result right away of skipping the Word, either. But in both cases, when you stop doing it, you get gradually weaker and weaker and you don't even know it for a while. Don't let that be you! Keep going.

2—Get Real

It's important to realize that every day isn't "goosebump day" when you read your Bible. Now, I've had times when I'm reading the Bible and it has the *exact* answer I need for my current problem or worry. Or times when a certain verse just *jumps* off the page at me and I have a super-revelation moment that changes everything.

But that's not every day. Some days I just read it. Some days it seems as dry as a bone. But 2 Timothy 3:16 says, *"All Scripture is given by inspiration of God, and is profitable for doctrine, for reproof, for correction, for instruction in righteousness."* It's all in the Bible for a reason, so I read it all. I want the full counsel of God, don't you? Not just the feel-good scriptures. It's all good. As I used to tell my students, if it sounds like bad news, read it again. Because it's all good. It's all profitable.

None of those "exact answer" days or those "super-revelation" days would ever have happened in my life if I wasn't reading the Bible. So I just read it every day. One person I know says, "If you wait for that 'good ol' Bible reading feeling' to come upon you before you read the Bible, you'll never read it!" That's why we want to make it a habit—something we do whether we feel like it or not.

3—Decide, Then Get Help

You have the power to make a quality decision in your life. No one will do it for you. But you *can* decide to be a daily Bible reader. I encourage you to say that out loud: "I'm a daily Bible reader." Write it down somewhere. Own it. Commit to it.

Then once you've done that, ask God for help! Don't you think He will help you develop a daily habit of getting to know Him better? Of learning and growing up spiritually? Of course He will! And once you've asked Him, ask some other Christians whom you know to help you. Ask them what *they* do for their daily devotions.

Ask them to partner with you. Statistics show that you have a better chance of following through with things—anything from exercise to eating right to developing a daily devotional habit—if you do it *with* someone. For one thing, it's just more fun, and more importantly, it keeps you accountable.

4—Find What Works for You

I once heard someone say that even though there are thousands of different exercises and exercise programs, this is the most effective one: *the one you'll do*. It's the same with a daily devotional habit! Don't set unrealistic goals for yourself—instead set yourself up for success.

If you're sharper in the evening than the morning, do your devotionals then. If lunch hour works best for you, great. If you like pretty things, set up a "devotional corner" with your favorite chair, decorations, and notebooks to make it a place you love. If you like coffee, treat yourself to a new brew that you drink while you're having your devotions.

If you don't love to read, download an audio Bible or use the YouVersion app instead (or watch it). Memorize key verses to get them down into your heart. I often take one scripture from my daily reading that stood out to me, write it on a card, and carry it around with me so I can meditate on it during the day (you can do it on your phone, too). One person I know puts scriptures in their daily reminders, so it pops up periodically during the day and they can stop and think about it.

I recommend reading through the Bible every year. There are a lot of different programs you can use in order to do that (just type "Bible reading programs" into your search engine and you'll see!). I use one that's in the front of my Bible, but the whole point is that I just do better when there is a prescribed plan to follow.

#3 Pray

Now that you've praised God and read your Bible, this is a good time to pray. There are many different kinds of prayer—I highly recommend a book called *Bible Prayer Study Course* by Kenneth E. Hagin to learn all the different kinds of prayer and how to pray them effectively.

But in your morning devotional time of prayer, remember that prayer is first and foremost a two-way conversation—it's talking *and* listening. Prayer is a privilege—it's your powerful contact with the greatest force in the universe. What a blessing it is that our God gives us direct access to Him 24 hours a day and loves it when we come to Him in prayer.

Prayer time during your devotions is a good time to ask God for the things you need, but remember, you don't want to do all the talking—you want to be sure you listen for (and *expect to hear)* His answers.

I pray for a variety of things during my devotional time. I'll pray for my own needs, and also for other people. I used to keep a long list of people I was praying for, but it got to be a burden. So now I just ask the Holy Spirit who needs prayer today, and let their names rise up in my spirit. (I actually do that all day long—I don't "carry over" or wait for my devotional prayer time when God brings someone to my heart. I'll just pray for them right then.)

This is also the time I'll bring my own needs before God and ask for His wisdom about things going on with me. I'm also diligent to cast every care on Him, trusting that He's working on my behalf.

There's one prayer I pray every single day: "Father, today put me in the right place at the right time, with the right people doing the right thing. Make me a blessing."

I think it's a great idea to keep a prayer journal of things you've asked for and people you've prayed for, so you can look back and see how God faithfully answered you. It will encourage you to keep praying! There's really nothing more exciting than seeing your prayers answered.

He's Bending Down to Hear You

The Bible says you can have utter confidence that God is listening to you when you pray. Psalm 40:1 says, *"I waited patiently for the Lord; and He inclined to me, and heard my cry,"* and Psalm 116:2 says, *"Because He has inclined His ear to me…I will call upon Him as long as I live."*

You know what I picture when I read that God "inclined to me"? I see Him *leaning forward* from His throne, bending down toward me so that He can hear every word, every prayer. The New Living Translation of the Bible says it this way in Psalm 116:2: *"Because he bends down to listen, I will pray as long as I have breath!"* Picture Him *bending down* to hear you. That's how closely He's paying attention—that's how much He wants to hear what you have to say.

In the New Testament, First John 5:14-15 says:

> *This is the confidence that we have in Him, that if we ask anything according to His will, He hears us. And if we know that He hears us, whatever we ask, we know that we have the petitions that we have asked of Him.*

How can you know that God is answering your prayers and paying attention to your situation? Because *He hears you!* He's paying close attention—the Bible says so.

Imagine what it would be like to pray to a God who wasn't listening, who didn't hear you. That would be a hopeless feeling, wouldn't it? You couldn't believe your prayers were being answered. Some people feel that way. They feel as if God isn't listening to them or paying any attention to them.

But the Bible shows us that isn't true, doesn't it? We can have confidence that He'll answer us every time we call on Him or ask for His direction. God's got you covered.

Make Prayer a Lifestyle

Even though we're talking here about daily devotional time, I have to mention that prayer shouldn't just be limited to this one time per day. We should pray all day long—be in constant contact with our heavenly Father.

In a letter to the Thessalonians, the apostle Paul tells us to *"pray continually"* (1 Thess. 5:17 NIV). In Philippians 4:6 he said, *"Do not be anxious about anything, but in every situation, by prayer and petition, with thanksgiving, present your requests to God"* (NIV). Talking to God should be something we do every day to sharpen our spiritual walk and deepen our connection to God.

Prayer doesn't just meet your needs and protect you; it shapes your world, your personality, and your responses to life's troubles. Prayer is how you keep God in the center of whatever is going on in your life, and how you invite Him to move in your circumstances.

The enemy expects you to pray only when things are going wrong, and then to neglect prayer when everything's going fine. So when you pray all the time and make prayer a lifestyle no matter what is happening in your life, you surprise the enemy. I don't know about you, but I like to keep the enemy off balance! He is a defeated foe, and I like to keep him in his place.

Knowing Him Changes the Way You Pray

The closer you get to God, the more it changes your prayer life. The more you know Him, the more you trust Him, and you don't beg in prayer—you don't say, "Oh please oh please help me!" No, when you know how much He loves you and how He has yearned for you to come to Him and spend time, you being to pray like this: "Thank You, Father, for Your love! Of course You want to help me and heal me and prosper me! You said so in Your Word, and I'm Your beloved child!"

God wants to sit down with you in the morning and hear what's on your heart. In the evening He wants to sit down with you at dinner and hear about your day. He's a friend you can talk to every morning and all day long. He wants to go everywhere you go. He wants to sit with you when you're quiet, rejoice with you in your victories, be with you every day, every step of the way.

You are His beloved child, and like any good Father He wants to spend time with you. He enjoys being with you! You can tell Him everything and ask Him anything. He is grateful for your company. After all, He created you for His pleasure: *"Thou art worthy, O Lord, to receive glory and honour and power: for thou hast created all things, and for thy pleasure they are and were created"* (Rev. 4:11 KJV).

The more you come to know Him and how much He loves you, the more you'll be able to believe Him. You can't really fully trust someone until you know them better—until you have some history together.

For example, let's say you needed some money, and I told you, "Call my dad—he'll be happy to loan you some money." Now, you don't know my dad, so you probably wouldn't call someone you don't know to ask for money. Or, you might be just desperate enough to do it, but even if you got brave and did it, you wouldn't know for sure that my dad would loan you the money. Why? Because you don't know him. You would *hope* he might give you the money, but you just couldn't be sure.

But what if I were to call as ask him for money? His one and only daughter, the apple of his eye. I *know* he'd give me the money. Why? Because I know him. I've been knowing him all my life. I've spent endless hours with him. We have history. As a result, I know what he would do in a given situation. Precedence has been set.

It's the same with God. The more time you spend with Him, the more you'll come to know Him, and the more you'll be able to trust Him, because you'll know how He reacts in all sorts of situations.

#4 Pray in the Spirit

Once you've expressed your needs and desires in your native language, spend some time praying in tongues. God has given us this amazing, supernatural, empowering, life-altering gift that you want to make use of every day of your life. Praying in tongues is a game-changer on every level.

I get so excited when talking about praying in tongues! It changed my life and it can change yours too—for the better. I want you to know more about this wonderful gift of power from God and get excited about it!

Here are six ways that praying in tongues can benefit you:

1. **It equips you with power.** When Jesus appeared to His disciples after He had risen from the tomb, the main thing He wanted them to know about was the baptism of the Holy Spirit. He said, *"I will send the Holy Spirit upon you, just as my Father promised...stay here in the city until the Holy Spirit comes and fills you with power from heaven"* (Luke 24:49 TLB). That same power is available to all believers today! If there's anything you and I need in these last days, it's God's power equipping us for every challenge.

2. **It reveals things to you.** The Holy Spirit's main ministry to us as believers is revelation, revealing God's will to us. Paul said, *"Eye has*

not seen, nor ear heard, nor have entered into the heart of man the things which God has prepared for those who love Him. But God has revealed them to us through His Spirit" (1 Cor. 2:9-10). We can know what God has prepared for us by praying in the spirit. I remember when I met the man who was to become my second husband. There was something about him that drew me to him, but what do we really know about another person? Everyone puts their best foot forward at a first meeting or on a date, but we can't really know what someone is like inside and whether they would make a good mate. So I prayed in the spirit, asking God to reveal the man's true nature, and also His true plan for my life. I'm so glad I did! After several weeks of praying in other tongues, I knew beyond a shadow of a doubt that I should marry this man, and we've been living happily ever after ever since!

3. **It builds you up and refreshes you.** Jude 20 says we can "build ourselves up" by praying in the spirit and First Corinthians 14:4 says, *"He who speaks in a tongue edifies himself."* Some synonyms of the word *edify* are elevate, enrich, uplift, improve, regenerate, renew, and transform. I love those words—I get refreshed just reading them. Isaiah 28 calls praying in tongues *"the refreshing"* (Isa. 28:12)!

4. **It gives you a hotline to God.** When you pray in tongues, no one understands it except God. You're talking right to Him; nothing is intercepting or scrambling the conversation. First Corinthians 14:2 says, *"He who speaks in a tongue does not speak to men but to God, for no one understands him; however, in the spirit he speaks mysteries."* The future is a mystery to us, right? But God knows the future. When we pray in tongues, we're praying right to Him, praying out the future, so that by the time we get there many things have already been set up for us.

5. **It helps you pray when you're stumped.** Romans 8:26 says, *"We do not know what we should pray for as we ought, but the Spirit Himself makes intercession for us."* Have you ever been in a situation where you didn't know what to pray? I have! You and I have limited knowledge about what's going on all around us in the spirit realm or in the future. But the Holy Spirit has all knowledge about it. When we pray in the Spirit, we're letting Him pray for the perfect outcome of any situation.

6. **It makes you bold.** In Acts 1:8 Jesus said, *"You shall receive power when the Holy Spirit has come upon you; and you shall be witnesses to Me in Jerusalem, and in all Judea and Samaria, and to the end of the earth."* I used to be less

than bold when it came to witnessing; I did not have the power to be a witness, neither in Jerusalem nor in all Judea and Samaria—or even in my neighborhood grocery store! But since I've fostered a habit of praying in tongues, it's taken the "chicken" out of me and I've gotten much bolder. The compassion of Jesus rises up in me, and I no longer care what anyone thinks. I'm able to be a bold witness for Him. You can too!

If you don't pray in tongues and you want to, now that you've read all those benefits, turn to the back of the book and read the page marked "How to Be Filled with the Holy Spirit." Then come on back here and keep reading.

#5 Make the Day's Schedule

Now that you've cozied up to God, spent time thanking Him, reading His Word (which filled your heart with faith), talking with Him, listening to Him, and releasing the power of the Holy Spirit, you're ready to plan your day! This is the best time to map out your course for the day (or for the next day, if you do your devotions at night), asking God to help you every step of the way.

When you do things in His strength and power, you are more effective and much less stressed. He knows exactly how to map out your time.

Here's what I've learned: when you put God first time-wise, He somehow can take that effort and *make extra time for you.* Now, of course, He doesn't really add hours to your day—you're not going to suddenly get a 26-hour day while the rest of us are trying to operate in a 24-hour day.

But when you put Him first, He can make the whole rest of your day run smoothly, and you end up getting way more done. You can enjoy His presence as you tackle potentially stressful events, and even be peaceful doing it (which is priceless).

Matthew 6:33 says it this way, *"Seek first the kingdom of God and His righteousness, and all these things shall be added to you."* I take that literally! Seek Him first—before anything else. I've found that when I put Him first, He makes sure I have everything I need to equip for the day.

You know as well as I do that there are endless delays and problems and snafus that can highjack our time and totally destroy even the best laid schedule. Somehow, when you let God have first crack at your time, He manages to put things in order so that everything goes much more smoothly. He redeems the time (see Eph. 5:15-16).

I don't know how He does it, but this is the same God who stopped the sun for Joshua (see Josh. 10:13) so it's not hard for Him to order time. It's supernatural, and it works! When you put Him first, listen to His voice, and walk close to Him, He can set things wonderfully in order.

It Happened to Me

I'll give you an example from my own life. My 85-year-old dad and I both love baseball, and not long ago we met up in Phoenix, Arizona to watch some spring training games.

He flew in from Oregon and I flew in from Minnesota to Phoenix Sky Harbor airport, which is *huge*.

You can imagine the logistics of finding each other in the airport, getting our respective luggage from different baggage claim areas, walking miles to the rental car shuttle area, catching the shuttle, renting the car, then navigating the drive to our hotel in Scottsdale—and then doing it all over again on the way back! Traveling is so glamorous, isn't it?

The trip coming into Phoenix went fine, although there were some bumps (and a *really* long bus ride from the airport to the car rental place). The whole process was tiring for my dad, even though we made it fine. We had a great four days watching baseball games, seeing the sights, and soaking up the sunshine.

On the morning we were leaving to fly home, I admit that I was feeling a little anxious and rushed—one of those times when you're tempted to think, "I don't have time to read the Bible and pray today." But I've learned that those are the times when you need to the most! Those are the days when you need God's up-close guidance and presence— and when He wants to help you every step of the way. I've heard Him whisper, "Karen, if you'll put Me first, I'll order your day." And I've seen Him do it again and again.

I had decided that I was just going to drop my dad off at the airport that morning and take the rental car back (and the shuttle) by myself, so he didn't have to endure that part of the journey. To be honest, though, I was a little nervous about the whole process, just because there were so many moving parts and so many things that could go wrong.

For example, my dad hadn't been sleeping well in his hotel room and I hoped he could get up and packed on time. Also, we had to head toward the airport during morning rush hour, so of course there could have been any kind of traffic problems imaginable.

Then there was the detail of dropping my dad off at departures by himself so he could check his bag, go through security and find his gate—all of that could be fraught with peril. *Then* I had to try and find the rental car return place from there, which is at least five miles away from the airport. Not to mention waiting for a shuttle bus back to the airport, then going through the baggage check and security lines myself.

So obviously, I prayed about it, and my husband prayed with me about it on the phone. I spent time with God that morning, thanking Him for His help and His assisting angels on duty every step of the way. Every time I thanked Him, I could feel His peace enveloping me. There was such a sense of "doing this together." No need to worry—I'd spent time with Him and as a result I knew He was with us, He was guiding us, He was paving the way.

And of course, that's just what happened. Dad was up early and ready to go an hour early! Thank You, Lord. Driving to the airport, we had no trouble at all with traffic—no delays at all. Thank You, Lord. Then even though it was crowded at the airport departure drop-off area, I was able to stop, get my dad's luggage out of the trunk, hug him, and send him on his way. Thank You, Lord.

Then as I drove away, there was a sign *right there* leading me to rental car return! The signage was great for the whole five miles, and just as I dropped the car without incident and headed for the shuttle stop, the bus to my terminal pulled up, ready to take me to the airport. Thank You, Lord.

Inside the terminal, every airline had a *huge* line to check baggage—except mine! Thank You, Lord. I got in line behind about four people, checked in in minutes, and headed off to security—where there was another *huge* line, except I had TSA pre-check and there was no line there and I was through security in minutes! Thank You, Lord.

Later, even though the concourse where my gate was located was crammed with people, I was able to find a quiet place in the next concourse over to sit and work until my flight. Thank You, Lord. As I sat looking out the window in my quiet spot, I thanked God all over again. It was actually *fun* to walk it all out with Him, thanking Him every step of the way and watching Him just set everything in order.

Having God order your steps each day is just one of the benefits of walking closely with Him. And I think He enjoyed it as much as I did!

The quality time you spend with God is vital to your relationship with Him. Forming a daily habit of spending time with Him will reap great benefits in your life! You don't have to do it the way I do—I've just given you these points as an example. But do your best to keep your daily appointment with Him. It's how you'll get closer and closer to His heart.

Review in a Nutshell

The way you get to know someone is by spending quality time with them, and the same is true of God. Daily devotional time—staying connected to the power source—is how you get to know God on a deeper level.

Now Engage:

Read and meditate the scriptures we've looked at, and activate the power of God's Word in your life by speaking these declarations out loud.

Be still, and know that I am God (Psalm 46:10).

Declare:

"When I am still in God's presence it helps me to overcome the mind-numbing flow of worldly information and to be intimately and securely anchored in my relationship with Him. When I'm still, I'm in a better position to hear from God."

Come to Me, all who are weary and burdened, and I will give you rest. Put My yoke upon your shoulders—it might appear heavy at first, but it is perfectly fitted to your curves. Learn from Me, for I am gentle and humble of heart. When you are yoked to Me, your weary souls will find rest. For My yoke is easy, and My burden is light (Matthew 11:28-30 VOICE).

Declare:

> "God is ready and willing to spend all the time in the world with me. He knows I'll be better off from having done it. That is an invitation I never want to turn down. God has given me an open invitation, 24/7, to come and spend time in His presence. To tell Him my worries and leave them in His capable hands. To get His wisdom and perspective on problems. To refuel, reboot, and renew my soul."

It is good to give thanks to the Lord, and to sing praises to Your name, O Most High; to declare Your lovingkindness in the morning, and Your faithfulness every night (Psalm 92:1-2).

Declare:

> "I will spend daily devotional time with my heavenly Father. It's the way I'll get to know Him better, walking in that close intimacy that He wants and I crave. I'll do whatever I can to carve out this wonderful, personal time with God. Everything hinges on it. It's not a duty— it's a joy."

In everything give thanks; for this is the will of God in Christ Jesus for you (1 Thessalonians 5:18).

Declare:

"I will praise and thank God for all He's done for me. He's saved me, healed me, bought me back from death and hell, made every provision for me, and given me His love, peace, and joy. He's made a home for me in heaven where I'll live forever, ruling and reigning with Him! He's always paying attention to every detail of my life, working all things together for my good when I ask Him to."

I will give thanks to you, Lord, with all my heart; I will tell of all your wonderful deeds (Psalm 9:1 NIV).

Declare:

"Every day I have a choice to thank God. No matter how dark things look, there is always something to thank Him for. Praising Him releases the supernatural power of God. When I praise Him, it gives me hope, and then faith, that I'm going to come out on top."

Heaven and earth will pass away, but My words will by no means pass away (Matthew 24:35).

Declare:

"The Bible is God talking to me—it's His will for me. It's where I find out who I am, and how to live a life of victory. The Bible is my anchor—the foundation of my life. There's no way to live the supernatural kind of life that Jesus died to give me, or get to know Him intimately, without reading His Word. I can't separate God from His Word."

Blessed be the God and Father of our Lord Jesus Christ, who has blessed us with every spiritual blessing in the heavenly places in Christ (Ephesians 1:3).

Declare:

"I don't read the Bible in order to be a 'good Christian' or to receive God's blessings. I've already received every blessing in Christ! I read the Bible to see what those blessings are and to keep them in the forefront of my mind so I can contend for them in everyday life. I read it so I know what belongs to me—to hear God's voice and follow His path. The Bible is God's instruction manual for my life."

I waited patiently for the Lord; and He inclined to me, and heard my cry (Psalm 40:1).

Declare:

"I know that God is listening to me when I pray. He is *leaning forward* from His throne so that He can hear every word, every prayer.

That's how closely He's paying attention—that's how much He wants to hear what I have to say."

Pray without ceasing (1 Thessalonians 5:17).

Declare:

"I will pray all day long and be in constant contact with my heavenly Father. Talking with Him all day sharpens my spiritual walk and deepens my connection with Him. Prayer is how I keep God in the center of whatever is going on in my life and how I invite Him to move in my circumstances."

I will send the Holy Spirit upon you, just as my Father promised...stay here in the city until the Holy Spirit comes and fills you with power from heaven (Luke 24:49 TLB).

Declare:

"Praying in tongues equips me with power, reveals God's truths to me, builds me up and refreshes me, helps me pray out the future, makes me bold, and can heal my body. What an amazing supernatural, empowering, life-altering gift God has given me. I will make use of it by praying in tongues daily."

Seek first the kingdom of God and His righteous-ness, and all these things shall be added to you (Matthew 6:33).

Declare:

"When I seek God first, He can take that effort and make my whole day run smoothly. As a result, I'll get more done. I can enjoy His presence as I tackle potentially stressful events, and even be peaceful doing it, which is priceless. When I put Him first, He makes sure I have everything I need to equip me for the day."

Discussion Questions:

Do you have a daily devotion time? If yes, what does it look like? What do you do to stay consistent? If no, do you want to now that you've read this chapter? Why or why not?

Chapter Seven

LIVING THE
ULTIMATE LIFE

JUST THE OTHER DAY I WAS STRUGGLING WITH SOME THINGS in my life and my head was all tangled up in the wrong place. Things weren't going the way I expected, people were bugging me, and I felt stuck. I was facing something that I just didn't want to do, and a gloom sort of settled on me like a wet blanket.

I was about an hour into my self-hosted pity party, when all of a sudden the words I had read from Psalm 136 during my morning devotions popped into my mind: *"Oh, give thanks to the Lord, for He is good! For His mercy endures forever."*

If you've ever read that Psalm, you know it has 26 verses and every single verse ends with the words "His mercy endures forever." It can be a little redundant while you're reading it, but if God says something that many times, I think He's trying to get a point across! At the time I read it, I was a little impatient and the words just seemed to bounce off of me, but when they came back to me later during my pity party, all of a sudden they went off in my spirit like—wow! His mercy endures *forever!* He is so good! Everything is going to be okay! Wow!

It's hard to describe spiritual things in natural words, but all I can say is—it was definitely a wonderful moment. God's joy coursed through me, the gloom lifted, and I was filled with the knowledge that I would not only survive this day, but I would come through with flying colors—I was on the victory side! Nehemiah 8:10 says, *"the joy of the Lord is your strength"*—I was filled with God's strength and I could do nothing but praise Him. I knew everything was going to work out fine.

Benefits of Being Close to God

I tell you that story to illustrate the fact that time spent with God—getting to know Him better and better—is never wasted, even if it doesn't seem like it at the time. Those words I'd hidden in my heart came back to me when I needed them the most. My time of drawing near to God helped solidify our intimacy, just as it does every day, whether I feel it at the time or not.

When you and I walk every day in close, intimate fellowship with God, we're really living the ultimate life. Just think of it—walking side by side with the Creator of the universe, tapping into the wisdom of the ages, hearing directly from the Source to fulfill our divine destiny, being unconditionally loved by the Lover of our souls and a blessing to everyone we meet—this is the ultimate life God has for us!

Psalm 16:1-11 gives us such a good picture of that life. There are so many benefits to knowing God and having a deep relationship with Him—here are just a few.

Verse 1 says that when we know Him, we are protected: *"Keep me safe, my God, for in you I take refuge"* (Ps. 16:1 NIV). In today's violent, volatile world, there's nothing better than knowing that He's watching over us and we are safe in Him.

Verse 3 tells us that knowing Him means we're not alone—we know fellow believers who have the same kind of relationship with Him that we do, and we can delight in growing together in Him: *"As for the saints who are on the earth, 'They are the excellent ones, in whom is all my delight'"* (Ps. 16:3).

Verses 5-6 show us a bright future in Him: *"Lord, you are my portion and my cup of blessing; you hold my future. The boundary lines have fallen for me in pleasant places; indeed, I have a beautiful inheritance"* (Ps. 16:5-6 CSB). When David wrote this psalm, his life was full of trouble, but he knew and trusted God, so he was joyfully content. Knowing God means we can praise Him no matter where we are and look forward with faith.

Verses 7-8 remind us how faithful God is to guide us: *"I will bless the Lord who counsels me—even at night when my thoughts trouble me. I always let the Lord guide me. Because he is at my right hand, I will not be shaken"* (Ps. 16:7-8 CSB). We don't have to worry or be shaken. What a firm foundation we have in Him!

Verses 9-11 indicate the wonderful promise we have of victory on this earth and then spending eternity with Him: *"Therefore my heart is glad, and my glory rejoices; my flesh also will rest in hope. For You will not leave my soul in Sheol, nor will You allow Your Holy One to see corruption. You will show me the path of life; in Your presence is fullness of joy; at Your right hand are pleasures forevermore."* There is such a peace in knowing our ultimate destination.

Close to the Healer

I recently received a testimony from a woman whose husband had been suffering from Parkinson's disease, and she had asked me a few weeks before to pray for him. Here's a portion of what she sent to me:

> I don't know how to say thank you enough. Recently, I asked that you include my husband, who has Parkinson's, on your prayer list. Since then, his physical battle has turned around significantly. Instead of being listless and depressed, he has been acting more like his "old self"—energetic, participating in church activities again, back to gardening and doing outdoor things—living a better, happier life. His meds also seem to be working better. "Miracle" doesn't seem like a strong enough word. I just can't thank you enough for your prayers.

As I read this precious woman's note, I thought, "What a benefit it is to know God!" This man was probably told that there was little hope for him in the medical world—but look at what God did! I was someone far away who wasn't really close with this man and his wife, but when I agreed with them (and probably others) in prayer for him, the Lord heard and answered us!

When we know Him, we are right up close to the Healer. We are not like those without Christ, without hope and help (see Eph. 2:12). We can expect our Father's love and healing power to overcome the trials and troubles that come our way.

Walking closely with Him gives us an advantage in every realm of life. Yes, it takes spiritual effort to spend time in His presence, to resist temptation, to live a life that pleases God. Romans 12:1 says, *"I beseech you therefore, brethren, by the mercies of God, that you present your bodies a living sacrifice, holy, acceptable to God, which is your reasonable service."* Some may think the sacrifice of laying down our lives to receive more of His is too much to ask (see Mark 8:34-35). But it's not! It's reasonable, the Bible says, and besides, the rewards are so much greater than any sacrifice we ever have to make.

Your Light Shines

Have you ever noticed that you can tell when someone knows God? It shines out of them! Matthew 5:16 says, *"Let your light so shine before men, that they may see your good works and glorify your Father in heaven."* The more you know God, the more He shines out of you. His peace, His joy, His confidence shows in your face and in your manner.

In Acts 4, Peter and John were arrested for preaching the Gospel. When it came time to defend themselves before the High Priest, Peter gave such a compelling and anointed testimony that it says, *"Now when they saw the boldness of Peter and John, and perceived that they were uneducated and untrained men, they marveled. And they realized that they had been with Jesus"* (Acts 4:13). It was evident to everyone in the place that day that Peter and John had been intimately acquainted with Jesus. Their boldness and confidence shone out of them.

The world needs people of faith today more than ever—they are drawn to the light in you. You see, we aren't trying to get closer to God so that we feel superior in a "I know Him and you don't!" kind of way. If anything, we get more humble when we are closer to Him. But aside from the benefits we receive from knowing Him, it makes our light shine!

Intimacy with God is for our benefit, but it's also for the benefit of others. If I can say it this way: the more you fill up with God and walk closely to Him, the more attractive you are to other people.

People can tell when we've spent time with God. Just like they can tell if we're living a superficial Christian life—maybe going to church, but just going through the motions; maybe talking the talk, but not walking the walk. That's what happens when we know *about* God but we don't *know Him* intimately, the way He wants to be known by us. And it's not fooling anyone.

What a blessing it is to genuinely know Him. It's a blessing in our individual life, and it's a blessing to everyone around us. A person who lives *full to the brim* of God's love and presence and power is truly living the ultimate life.

Review in a Nutshell

Walking with God every day in close, intimate fellowship is living the ultimate life, and it's the life God wants for you.

Now Engage:

Read and meditate the scriptures we've looked at, and activate the power of God's Word in your life by speaking these declarations out loud.

> *Oh, give thanks to the Lord, for He is good! For His mercy endures forever* (Psalm 13:1).

Declare:

> "Walking side by side with the Creator of the universe, tapping into the wisdom of the ages, hearing directly from the Source to fulfill my divine destiny, being unconditionally loved by the Lover of my soul and a blessing to everyone I meet—this is the ultimate life God has for me!"

> *Keep me safe, my God, for in you I take refuge* (Psalm 16:1 NIV).

Declare:

> "When I know God and walk closely with Him, I am protected. In today's violent, volatile world, there's nothing better than knowing

that He's watching over me and I am safe in Him."

As for the saints who are on the earth, "They are the excellent ones, in whom is all my delight" (Psalm 16:3).

Declare:

"Knowing God means I'm not alone—I know fellow believers who have the same kind of relationship with Him that I do, and together we can delight in growing in Him."

Lord, you are my portion and my cup of blessing; you hold my future. The boundary lines have fallen for me in pleasant places; indeed, I have a beautiful inheritance (Psalm 16:5-6 CSB).

Declare:

"I have a bright future! Even in times of trouble, I trust God because I know Him. I am joyfully content and praise Him in every circumstance. I look forward with faith because I have a beautiful inheritance."

I will bless the Lord who counsels me—even at night when my thoughts trouble me. I always let the Lord guide me. Because he is at my right hand, I will not be shaken (Psalm 16:7-8 CSB).

Declare:

> "God is faithful to counsel and guide me. I won't worry—I cannot be shaken! What a foundation I have in Him."

> *Therefore my heart is glad, and my glory rejoices; my flesh also will rest in hope. For You will not leave my soul in Sheol, nor will You allow Your Holy One to see corruption. You will show me the path of life; in Your presence is fullness of joy; at Your right hand are pleasures forevermore* (Psalm 16:9-11).

Declare:

> "Because I know God, my heart is glad and I rejoice. I rest in hope. God shows me the path of life. I have victory on this earth and then get to spend eternity with Him!"

> *I beseech you therefore, brethren, by the mercies of God, that you present your bodies a living sacrifice, holy, acceptable to God, which is your reasonable service* (Romans 12:1).

Declare:

> "Although it takes spiritual effort to spend time in God's presence, to resist temptation, and to live a life that pleases God, it's worth it! The sacrifice of laying down my life to receive more of His is not too much to ask. It's reasonable,

and besides, the rewards are so much greater than any sacrifice I ever have to make."

Let your light so shine before men, that they may see your good works and glorify your Father in heaven (Matthew 5:16).

Declare:

"People can tell that I know God. It shines out of me! The more I know God, the more His peace, His joy, and His confidence show in my face and in my manner. The more I fill up with God and walk closely to Him, the more attractive I am to other people."

Now when they saw the boldness of Peter and John, and perceived that they were uneducated and untrained men, they marveled. And they realized that they had been with Jesus (Acts 4:13).

Declare:

"When I am intimately acquainted with Jesus, it will be evident. People can tell when I've spent time with God—my boldness and confidence will shine out."

Discussion Questions:

Do you believe God wants you to live the ultimate life? What, if anything, do you think might be holding you back from it? What do you need to change to live the ultimate life?

ASK JESUS TO BE YOUR SAVIOR

YOU MAY BE READING THIS BOOK BECAUSE YOU WANT TO GET closer to God. Good for you—He wants to get closer to you too! The first step is to receive His Son, Jesus, and your own personal Lord and Savior. You can't get closer to Him if you've never met the God who holds your future.

I want to invite you into a relationship with Him. Asking Jesus to be your Savior is the most important decision you'll ever make. It's the starting point for getting your life on the right track. You can't understand any of the principles in the Bible, or in this book, until you've started a relationship with Jesus by asking Him into your heart.

There came a time in my life when I had to make a decision to receive Jesus—just like anyone who is a Christian has had to do. I can sincerely say that if it wasn't for Him being in my life I wouldn't be where I am today. We all are born into sin, according to Romans 3:23: *"For everyone has sinned; we all fall short of God's glorious standard"* (NLT). Sin separates you, me, everyone from God.

But 2,000 years ago, God sent Jesus—His only Son— to the earth as a man to die on the Cross and bear the consequences of our sin so we could be restored to a perfect relationship or "right standing" with God:

> *"He himself bore our sins" in his body on the cross, so that we might die to sins and live for righteousness* (1 Peter 2:24 NIV).

Jesus traded places with us—He actually became sin so that we could become righteous in God's eyes:

> *God made him who had no sin to be sin for us, so that in him we might become the righteousness of God* (2 Corinthians 5:21 NIV).

God loves you, not because you've done everything right or because you're good, but because *He* is good. He loves you so much that He sent Jesus to pay a price for you that you could never pay. He did this because He wants to have a one-on-one, day-by-day, personal relationship with you.

It is God's will for you to be saved. It's the first step in His plan for your life. If you've never received Jesus as your Savior, then you've never received the benefits of what He did for you on the Cross. You are still in a sinful state. You're not yet in a position to receive His help for making the decisions of your life.

But you can receive Him *today.* It's not hard.

The Bible says that *"if you confess with your mouth the Lord Jesus and believe in your heart that God has raised Him from the dead, you will be saved"* (Rom. 10:9). All God's blessings and benefits of salvation can be yours if you receive Him into your heart.

Jesus died for you, but it's your decision—the most important decision of our life—to invite Him into your life.

Think of it like a guy jumping out of a plane with a parachute. Everything goes fine for a while, but unless he makes the decision to pull the rip cord, things are going to turn out badly for him. I encourage you today—pull the cord! You can do it by praying this prayer:

> *Dear God, I come to You admitting that I am a sinner. I believe that Your Son, Jesus, died on the Cross to take away my sin. I also believe He rose from the dead so I can be justified and made righteous through faith in Him. Jesus, I choose to follow You, and I ask that You fill me with the power of the Holy Spirit. Thank You for saving me! Amen.*

Congratulations, and welcome to the family of God! Now you are born again—you're a new creation in Christ (see 2 Cor. 5:17). Next, you'll want to read the following pages about how to be filled with the Holy Spirit—because it's all part of the deal, and you might as well get the whole load right now!

If you prayed that prayer above for the first time, I'd like to hear from you so I can send you a special gift. Please contact me through my website listed on the About the Author page. I also encourage you to get into a good Bible-believing church so you can learn more about your faith and grow in your relationship with God.

HOW TO BE FILLED
WITH THE HOLY SPIRIT

IF YOU'VE NEVER RECEIVED THE BAPTISM OF THE HOLY SPIRIT with the evidence of speaking in tongues, it's time you did. It's not hard, and you don't have to qualify for it or earn it. Speaking in tongues is a free gift from God, for all His children, and it's just one of the best things that can ever happen to you!

God wants you to have this gift. If I were to walk up to you with a gift in my hands and say, "This is for you," what would you have to do to receive it? Would you have to pay me for it? Would you have to perform or beg in order to receive it? No. All you would need to do would be to reach out and take it, wouldn't you? That's all you have to do with this gift from God, too.

First, to be filled with the Holy Spirit, you must be born again:

Then Peter said to them, "Repent, and let every one of you be baptized in the name of Jesus Christ for the remission of sins; and you shall receive the gift of the Holy Spirit. For the promise is to you and to your children, and to all who are afar off, as many as the Lord our God will call" (Acts 2:38-39).

If you are not sure if you're born again, flip back a page or two and read "Ask Jesus to Be Your Savior" and pray the prayer you find there. Then come back here and keep reading.

The baptism of the Holy Spirit is received by faith, just as the new birth is received by faith. Jesus said in Luke 11:13, *"If you then, being evil, know how to give good gifts to your children, how much more will your heavenly Father give the Holy Spirit to those who ask Him!"* When you ask in faith, the Holy Spirit comes upon you, and you'll speak in tongues. It's as simple as that.

Notice I said it's *you* who will speak in tongues. It will be your tongue, your breath, and your vocal cords doing the talking. Simply yield your tongue to His use. You'll supply the sounds, and the Holy Spirit will supply the words. You'll be forming syllables around the expression that your heart desires to release. Speaking words unknown to you might seem awkward at first, but just keep practicing like a child learning to speak.

To receive the baptism in the Holy Spirit you don't need to "get a word from God" about it—you already have His

Word. You don't need to wait. The only waiting was done on the Day of Pentecost. The Holy Spirit came to Earth that day and He's been here ever since.

And you don't need to worry about being deceived and ending up with something that is from the devil. When you ask your heavenly Father for one of His promises, such as the baptism in the Holy Spirit, you can be confident the gift given is from God, not Satan.

If you're ready, just ask God right now. You could pray something like this:

> *Father, I'm a believer. Your Word says if I'll ask, I'll receive the Holy Spirit. So in the Name of Jesus, I'm asking You to baptize me in the Holy Spirit. Because of Your Word, I believe that I receive. Thank You! Now, Holy Spirit, rise up within me as I praise God. I fully expect to speak with other tongues, as You give me the utterance.*

Now begin to speak, giving voice to the expressions that rise up from your inner man. Speak and hear the Holy Spirit speaking through you. Praise God! You've just been baptized in the Holy Spirit, endowed with your heavenly Father's power. Now keep on speaking, and keep on practicing. Keep on tapping into the power! And if you got filled today, please contact me through my website (address on the following pages) because I have something I want to give you.

About
Karen Jensen Salisbury

 Karen Jensen Salisbury has been in ministry for almost 30 years and a writer for almost 40. She and her first husband, Brent, traveled as itinerant ministers and also pioneered two churches in the Northwest.

In 1997, upon Brent's unexpected death, she became senior pastor of their church in Boise, Idaho. She raised their sons, Josh and Ryan, through their teenage years into young men on fire for God.

Karen was an instructor at Rhema Bible Training College in Broken Arrow, Oklahoma from 2005 to 2014. In March of 2014 she married businessman Bob Salisbury, and they live in Minneapolis. Now in addition to writing books, Karen travels across the US and overseas, sharing what she has learned about the faithfulness of God through good times and bad.

Her teachings and writings have influenced the lives of hundreds of thousands of people all over the world. Her humor, her never-give-up attitude, her love for God, and her strong stand on His Word will bless and inspire you.

Visit Karen's Website

Visit Karen at her website, www.karenjensensalisbury.org, where you can:

- Contact her personally—she'd love to hear from you
- Book her for speaking engagements
- Shop for MP3s, CDs, DVDs, books, and more
- Watch videos of Karen
- Read her blogs, "Parenting With Faith" and "This Is the Life"
- Be encouraged by reading her archived teachings
- Follow her itinerary
- And more…

Let Karen Encourage You with God's Word

2-CD SERIES—If you're like most of us, you've had painful things happen to you. But God doesn't want you to stay hurt. Learn how to cut the chains of hurt and live a life of forgiveness.

3-CD SERIES—You've never been loved like this before! Learn more about how *you* are the focus of God's everlasting love and how believing and accepting that love will change your life in every way.

BOOK—Has something terrible happened in your life? Do you have questions for God? Here is a handbook for getting answers and getting past the pain.

Order these and other products from
www.karensalisbury.org

Help for Parents

Host A Parenting Seminar

Karen has conducted Parenting With a Purpose Seminars throughout the US and overseas. Her seminars cover both spiritual and practical aspects of parenting for both married and single parents.

Seminar topics include:

- God's plan for your family
- Surrounding your children with faith and love
- Obedience and correction
- Roles and stages of parenting

This seminar was far above everything I expected. It has equipped me with information that I needed to properly launch my children into their destinies.

—R.T.

Help and Advice for Raising Your Kids

These powerful and practical Bible-based lessons have helped families around the world. They can equip and encourage any parent, no matter the age of their child.

CD or DVD materials for personal or group use:

- Sixteen half-hour lessons
- Great for personal use or group study (cell groups, church classes, special meetings, community outreach)
- Workbooks and group leader workbook available
- Thirty-one-day devotional for parents

To schedule a seminar or order materials go to:
www.karensalisbury.org

Be part of Karen's team!

Nine ways you can help get the word out about this book

1) **Buy the books.** The sooner you buy, the more book sales will attract the attention of key decision makers among the media and consumers. Buy as many copies as you can, buy some for friends.

2) **Ask** for the books everywhere books are sold (both chains and privately owned stores) even if you already have them. This helps owners and managers to know there is interest in the books, and may just cause them to order it for their store.

3) **Help Karen get speaking and interview opportunities.** Recommend Karen to your church, conferences, women's groups, book clubs, and events—or anyone you know connected with the media: newspaper or magazine editors/reporters, radio producers or hosts, TV show producers or hosts, columnists, bloggers, etc. Send them copies of the book, or tell Karen about your connection and introduce her to them. See "Invite Karen" on her website, karensalisbury.org

4) **Recommend this website** (karensalisbury.org). Link it to your website, blog, Facebook page, etc. Tweet about it. When Karen writes a blog post, link to it. If she tweets something great, retweet it.

5) **Pray!** The goal of these books is to help as many people as possble. Pray for God's supernatural help in getting

them into the hands of everyone who needs them. (Matthew 21:22, Luke 11:10, John 16:24)

6) **Recommend the book.** If you like them, recommend them to friends. Talk about them, quote them, tell what you like about them. Share on your blog, Twitter, Facebook, with your reading club or church bookstore or to bookstores and specialty retailers in your town.

7) **Review the book. This is huge!** Do a video review and post it to YouTube or Vimeo. Or send your review to Karen via the contact page. Post reviews in blogs, book websites, social media, and especially Amazon (see below).

8) **Aim for Amazon.** Amazon is the big kahuna of book sellers, especially when it comes to e-books, so helping any author get found on it gives a big boost.

   - Write a review. Just a few sentences will do.
   - Tag the books with a "Religion & Spirituality" or "Christian" label. You don't have to leave a review to do this; you just need an account at Amazon. The right tags and a good sales ranking can make a book come up when customers search.
   - Give the books a thumbs up. Takes less than a second.
   - Make a Listmania or Goodreads list and add Karen's books to it. This creates another avenue for new readers to find it.

9) **Sell the book.** At your events, in your church bookstore, or your product table if you travel. Click here for discount information: http://karenjensen.org/index. php/store/bookstore-discounts

The Harrison House Vision

Proclaiming the truth and the power
of the Gospel of Jesus Christ with excellence.
Challenging Christians
to live victoriously,
grow spiritually,
know God intimately.